Tomorrow Died Yesterday

Tomorrow Died Yesterday:

A Survivor's Guide to the Loss of a Spouse

Kathleen J. Cahalan, PhD
and
John A. Cosco, PhD

C & C Paradox Publishing, LLC
Cincinnati, Ohio

No part of this book is intended to provide legal or financial advice, nor to substitute for therapy. Neither of us is an attorney, certified financial planner, or licensed therapist. Please consult a legal or financial professional or therapist to obtain advice for any issues you might have.

In the stories told within this book, names have been changed, or no names have been used, details of the stories have been removed or changed, and in some cases, stories have been combined, to protect identities.

ISBN-13: 978-1541080560
ISBN-10: 1541080564

Published by C & C Paradox Publishing, LLC
Cincinnati, Ohio

Printed in the United States of America

Front cover photograph © 2017 by John A. Cosco

To **Dennis**, healer, dancer, drummer, seeker, my love forever.

- *Kathy*

To **Nancy**, my life, my light, my love, and my soul mate;

To **Justin and Stephen** my heroes and my sons who pursued life with determination, integrity, courage and vigor; and,

To **Brigid, Chris, Danny, Matt, and Tim,** my five unborn angels;

Until we meet again and dance in the heavenly presence of Our Lord.

- *John*

Acknowledgements

Thanks to all the widows and widowers I met in grief support groups who shared their stories and their nonjudgmental empathy.

Thanks to those who read drafts of this book and offered many helpful suggestions.

Thanks to my friends and family who offered encouragement and suggestions during the writing of this book.

Thanks to my co-author for his openness to suggestions, his wisdom, his encouragement, and his creative collaboration.

I offer my heartfelt gratitude to those family and friends who supported me through the aftermath of Dennis's death. To those who helped me clean my house, who raked my leaves, who kept me company at difficult times, who listened to my story, who offered me solace during those first raw holidays, who pulled me into your family, who sent me messages on my birthday and on difficult anniversaries, or who called me every day, I thank you from the bottom of my heart.

- *Kathy*

No literary endeavor is completed solely by the authors. Many skilled and talented individuals are valuable collaborators who offer gentle suggestions and valuable inputs to help assure the relevancy and accuracy of content is on target for potential readers.

Special thanks to my co-author for insight, collaboration, and contributions in the development of this book.

For reading my drafts, offering constructive comments and overall willingness to be of assistance particular expressions of gratitude are extended to colleagues:

Dr. Joan Shirley, nationally known special educator, professor, author, clinical administrator, and advocate;

Dr. Jan Dyehouse, Professor Emeritus of Nursing, past Department of Nursing Chairperson and former Associate Dean for Academic Research, University of Cincinnati, professional consultant, nursing practitioner, and author; and,

Dr. Bonnie J. Miller, Professor Emeritus of Nursing and former Department of Nursing Chairperson, Xavier University, Cincinnati, Ohio, consultant, pastoral counselor, staff educator, author, nursing administrator, and nursing practitioner.

Special thanks to author Karen Kennedy for expert guidance, tips, and advice with regard to self-publishing.

Special thanks to members of support groups and friends who shared personal experiences, perspectives, inputs, comments, suggestions, and encouragement.

Thanks to everyone for support, encouragement, and patience.

- *John*

Table of Contents

Introduction

Kathy writes:

You have been ripped away from half of who you once were. You have lost your spouse, or your most significant other, to the final separation, death. You are desperate for something, anything, to ease the pain. All your plans are destroyed. Tomorrow died yesterday. Will the pain ever end? Will life ever be the same?

Or you want to understand this person whose partner has died. How can you help? Can you help? Is this normal?

Both of us, John and Kathy, the authors of this book, have lost a spouse. Each of us has some training in psychology, or counseling, or healing arts, but each of us has lost a spouse. We have gone through this devastating experience ourselves. We feel that only those who have actually gone through this experience can truly understand how it feels, what the difficulties are, and what those things are that have helped us heal. We have discovered that the journey is very individual, and that each person must find their own way towards healing, and in their own time. But we have also discovered common experiences, and suggestions we can make, based on what has worked for each of us. Each grieving person must decide what works for herself or for himself, but in this book we will share our experiences, and those of others whose stories we have heard.

John and I met in a widow and widowers' grief support group in 2014, and discovered that we shared an interest in lifelong study, and that we had even been in the same graduating class decades before. Soon we also discovered a common interest in writing, and decided to write a book together about our experiences in coping with the loss of a spouse.

John and I have much in common, but in some ways we have very different philosophies and spiritual practices. Views that John expresses in this book about his own beliefs and practices do not necessarily represent my belief or practices, and my own view does not necessarily represent his. We respect each other's differences, and each of us chooses not to proselytize. When we describe our stories in this book, it is not with the intent to prescribe what others should do or believe, but only to describe each story, with the hope that the reader will take from it what might work for that reader.

And so we hope that this book will help our readers to heal, in a very realistic way. We hope this book will touch on some topics rarely covered in grief books. We hope that you will discover something in this book to help you understand, to cope, and to heal.

This book is divided into five parts. In a sense, this organization is chronological, because each part focuses on events that generally tend to occur after the events of the previous part. However, we have discovered that grief is not a strict set of stages. For example, it is possible to experience an intense grief attack long after the initial stages of grief, or to engage in a coping strategy in the earliest stage. The organization of this book is for ease of reference only, and is not a suggestion about what is normal.

Part 1 describes the initial shock of the loss, some common experiences, and how those experiences might be different depending on the circumstances. In that section, John and I each tell the story of our own loss.

Part 2 describes the ceremonies and tasks that are thrust upon the grieving partner in the initial period after the loss – the funeral or memorial service, writing of an obituary, notifications, and financial transactions that must take place. This section offers suggestions and checklists for these duties that must be implemented during this time of shock, when the grieving partner is least able to cope in an efficient and effective way.

Part 3 describes the initial adjustment that takes place in the first weeks and months after the loss. This is a critical time when the loss is still so very fresh. This section describes both practical and emotional issues, but it also describes sources of strength and support.

Part 4 focuses on the shift that happens as the grieving person learns to cope with life without their partner. This section describes a variety of difficulties, some common and some unusual, and ways to cope and to heal.

Part 5 concentrates on the creation of a new life as the grieving person recovers from the initial shock and finds new ways to cope. This section covers new relationships, where to live, traveling, work, and decisions about the new identity chosen by the grieving person.

Following Part 5 is a section called "Resources". Although it appears at the end of this book, it is a very important section that might help you discover new ways to cope with loss. This section includes lists of hotlines, chat rooms, forums, support groups, conferences, websites both for widows and for friends of widows, books, articles, and film.

This book is for those who have lost a partner, not necessarily a spouse, and not necessarily the opposite gender. In some cases, we use the words "widow" or "widower" or "spouse", among other terms, but we hope that you will understand that the intent is to include all those who have suffered the loss of a partner.

Although this book might refer to legal and financial solutions we found useful, no part of this book is intended to provide legal or financial advice, nor to substitute for therapy. Neither of us is an attorney, certified financial planner, or licensed therapist. Please consult a legal or financial professional or therapist to obtain advice for any issues you might have.

This book refers to a few stories other than our own stories, to broaden the information provided. For those stories, names have been changed, or no names have been used, details of the stories have been removed or changed, and in some cases, stories have been combined, to protect identities.

John writes:

Death of a spouse shatters the fiber of one's being, knocking the widowed survivor off-center. Life will never be the same. Losing a spouse ranks among the most difficult tragedies a person will ever face. Widowhood heralds the termination of an extraordinary, intimate, perhaps a once in a lifetime wedded relationship for many. Sadly, the death of a spouse generally leaves a widowed survivor who faces an uncertain future and the possibility of spending the remainder of life alone. Hopefully survivors will eventually shed their sadness, devastation, and disorientation to begin walking toward the brightness of a future horizon.

Widowhood can mean a grief-stricken existence of excruciating loneliness and sequestration. However, surviving the death of a spouse can provide the aggrieved with opportunities for rediscovery, interpersonal growth, and self-renewal. Many cultures and religions teach death is not an ending, but a transition into a dimension of eternal life, tranquility, and happiness. Theoretically, death marks new beginnings for both the deceased and the widowed. But recovery and healing will take time.

Widowed survivors, at the death of their spouse, become pilgrims embarking on a grief journey. (For this book, "grief journey" marks the course or path followed by many widowed survivors after the passage of their spouse.) The grief journey begins whether the spouse's death occurred suddenly or from an extended terminal illness. Death swoops in and strikes with cold, relentless brutality, thereby casting the widowed survivor onto the path of a grief journey. A grief journey unleashes a constellation of countless emotions, moods, and feelings.

Each grief journey is a wild roller coaster ride with no destination, map, or itinerary. Survivors blaze different pathways, take personal side trips, and plot their own route.

Widowed survivors quickly feel stinging spiritual, mental, physical, and emotional turmoil. The mayhem of death causes survivors to face many grim realities within a very compacted timeframe. Shock causes some survivors to become stunned and possibly dysfunctional.

Death's powerful bite sets the stage for a production in which we will play both supporting and starring roles. Our parts in the drama have already been casted. There are no auditions or dress rehearsals. Freud proclaimed death is the end goal of all living creatures. We are all going to die. Death happens to all mortal creatures.

Death strikes spouses, children, family members, and friends. Death represents transitions, changes, new beginnings, terminations, and rebirths. We witness death daily. Seeds must grow, die, and be replanted to germinate and bear new fruit. This simple fact constitutes the life cycle.

Death also hides itself in routine, nondescript, inanimate objects like bus schedules, elections, airline routes, and work shifts -- anything subject to modification, revision, or change. People happily embrace some changes in the interests of progress, upgrading, or improvement.

Death can summon happiness, joy, growth, festivity, recovery, new beginnings, and independence. The birth of a child changes the parents' lifestyle, but they celebrate new life. Children marry and leave their parents, but encounter new beginnings with their spouse. A worker sheds old routines after a promotion, but welcomes new responsibilities, recognition, and increased income.

I have cautioned married relatives and friends that in each of their marriages one of them will most likely bear the crown of widowhood. An etching I read on a tombstone expressed, "As you are now, so once was I; as I am now, so you will be."

The deaths of my beloved spouse, two adult sons, and five unborn children haunt me daily. "Now I am alone!" is a painful realization permanently imprinted in my mind.

I personally believe my spiritual beliefs, prayers, and religious practices will sustain me. I know, with certainty, my beloved and I will reunite in a happier place beyond this worldly realm. I pray God grants you strength, wisdom, hope, and courage as you face a new future filled with healing, confidence, peace, and joy.

Four facts are irrefutable:
- Death is imminent.
- Love lasts forever.
- Grief is hard work.
- Growth, joy, and hope are possible again.

Kathy and I met through a widowed survivors support group. Early in our association we discovered we could intelligently and extensively converse on many subjects in great depth and detail. We are both wounded by the sudden, unanticipated deaths of our spouses. We have chatted about emotions, feelings, pains, stressors, and the challenges of "moving ahead" alone. Some of our views, outlooks, and beliefs coincide, and others differ.

As writers and widowed survivors, we concluded our stories and experiences needed to be shared. Some parts of our histories are similar and others are vastly divergent. We both understand the pains of widowed survivors whose spouses died suddenly. We are less familiar with the sufferings of survivors whose spouses died from prolonged, lingering illnesses and we need to learn more about their experiences.

I hope the views, experiences, and discussions contained in this book can become a resource for widowed survivors. This manuscript endeavors to aide survivors to find affirmation, healing, and realization they are not alone. I encourage readers to share their stories. Comments, input, and feedback are welcome.

Part 1. Initial Shock

Part 1 describes the initial shock just after the death of the partner. In the chapters of Part 1, as in all the chapters of this book, each of us (Kathy and John) takes a turn to tell our own perspective. We begin by each telling our own personal story. We discuss the differences between a sudden loss and a lingering illness, and describe the physical and emotional sensations that are common to the initial experience of loss. We describe some strategies that we used to cope with the intense experience just after this most traumatic loss.

1.1 Our Stories

Kathy writes:

I first met Dennis on a Friday night in September 1969. Years later, we both remembered that day in vivid detail, down to the clothes we were wearing. By coincidence or synchronicity, we both wore blue and white striped bell-bottom pants. He had black hair and a moustache, and eyes that were the darkest I had ever seen, but kind and with a twinkle of humor. He was soft-spoken but enthusiastic, and expressed interest in ideas that fascinated me, ideas that revolved around psychology and philosophy. He tried an experiment that night to find out if I would fall backwards into his arms. I just kept laughing and couldn't quite do it.

Despite our mutual attraction, I spent most of my time 100 miles away, at school. We remained good friends, but we both developed relationships with other people. I finished my degree in psychology, and then went on to get a master's degree in Montessori education.   I taught as a Montessori teacher for two years, and then returned to graduate school, where I obtained a master's degree in experimental psychology. In 1977, I discovered a strong interest in computer programming, and switched to that field, where I stayed for 35 years. Along the way, I got an MBA and PhD in information systems, and managed to combine aspects of education, psychology, and systems in my studies and my work.

But back in the 1970s, Dennis and I were friends for many years before we fell madly in love with each other. We were married in 1985, but we had felt married for years already. Together we danced, drummed, played harps, solved computer problems, helped each other through school, tracked in the wilderness, hiked, bicycled, and healed each other. We had planned finally to build a house on our 40 wooded acres an hour's drive from our suburban house, grow our own food, walk or bicycle every day, travel, and have great adventures when I would retire in early 2010.

But it was not to be. Suddenly, with no warning, he died in his sleep in October 2009. The day before, he had taken a long bicycle trip on the Little Miami Scenic Trail, and that evening we had visited a bookstore and talked about each other's new books. One minute everything was normal, and then the next minute he was gone. I felt as if half of me had been ripped away.

I realized when I wrote this obituary how much he had squeezed into his short lifetime, as if he knew it would not last long:

> Dennis Jacob Fausz, owner of the alternative healing practice Metta Wellness and a retired computer systems specialist, died on October 31, 2009 in Edgewood, Kentucky. He was 60.

> In his lifetime, Mr. Fausz mastered an impressive range of occupations and knowledge. "I have never known anyone with such diverse skills, talents, and interests,"

said his brother-in-law, James M. Cahalan of Indiana, Pa. "He was a very gifted and generous person."

Graduating in the top 10% of his high school class, Mr. Fausz was a National Merit Semifinalist. He was a talented singer who was accepted into the College Conservatory of Music at the University of Cincinnati, although he was not able to attend.

In 1969, he first met and befriended Kathleen Joy Cahalan, whom he married in 1985.

He worked as a union carpenter for close to a decade in the 1970s. From 1978 to 1980 he served as a volunteer on the life squad in Edgewood, Kentucky, and was certified as an Emergency Medical Technician (EMT) in 1980. In 1986, he completed a B.S. degree in computer science from Northern Kentucky University. Then he worked for 17 years as a computer science professional.

At the same time that he worked in the field of computer science, he developed a deep level of expertise in movement and healing arts. From 1983 to 1993, he performed as a dancer with the Flying Cloud Academy of Vintage Dance. He performed in *North and South I* and *North and South II*, which appeared on a major national television network, and in *Glory*, an academy-award-winning film, as well as many live stage performances. From 1989 to 1995, he taught Tango dancing. He founded the Cincinnati Argentine Tango Society (CATS) in 1991. In 1993, he travelled to Argentina to study tango. In the 1990s, Dennis also focused on West African and Afro-Caribbean drumming, and performed in the Kai Kweol Caribbean Music and Dance company. In 2001, he learned the basics of the Irish/Scottish wire harp, and chaired the performer committee for HarpCon 2003, an international harp conference held in Bloomington, Indiana.

Dennis received a certificate from the Cincinnati School of Hypnosis in 1989, and gave hypnotherapy sessions over the next two years. From 1995 to 1998, he studied energy healing with Rosalyn Bruyere. In 1998, he certified as a Reiki Master. He certified as a Chi-Lel Qigong Level-1 Instructor in 1999, and presented several workshops through 2002. He completed certification for Thai Yoga Therapy and for Trager Psychophysical Integration in 2004. In 2005, he started the Metta Wellness company, and continued to provide sessions in movement education and relaxation up until the time of his death.

So many people came to the memorial service that we had trouble gathering enough chairs. People described how Dennis would plunge whole-heartedly into everything he did. People spoke of his warm, nurturing nature. Dancers spoke about his taking the time to dance with newcomers when no one else would dance with them. Others spoke about the warmth, sincerity, and gratitude he radiated in his healing practice.

Dennis had been part of my life from the time I was 20 years old. We were the same age, just a month apart. He had become so much a part of me that it seemed our thoughts and feelings merged together. Often one of us would start singing a song that the other one had just been hearing inside.

He died suddenly and completely unexpectedly, just before we were about to retire and go on adventures together, at the age of 60, far too young. I was in shock and completely shattered. We had no children, and he was my best friend, so it felt as if I had lost my whole family. His death happened more than six years ago at this writing. I'm no longer in such shock at this point, but I am still recovering, even now.

In the beginning, the loneliness was so intense that I desperately reached out, trying to do anything to reduce the silence. I joined four different grief support groups, all at the same time. That was one of the best things I did. Dennis and I had been planning to build a house in a forest that we owned. That forest is my sanctuary, my center, the place where I could always go if everything fell apart around me, the source of my spiritual energy. So I have been trying to continue that dream. I am not sure how far I will get, but I am still trying.

What many widows have said about the loss of friendships resonates with me. I myself lost friendships after his death that I had thought were eternal. At first these friends were very supportive, but soon they drifted away. I have read that this is a common phenomenon for widows, but still it really hurt, especially coming on top of such a wrenching loss as the death of a spouse.

I'm still in the house we shared together, near the city where we worked, 50 miles away from the forest we owned. I need to downsize and will have to move from this house at some point. I have experienced some well-meaning people try to push these decisions faster than I am able to make them. For the most part, I have stood my ground, insisting that I must do things in my own time and in my own way.

Right after Dennis died, I cut back my work hours to part-time, and then retired in summer 2011. I spend my time now preparing to sell this house, trying to build something on the forest property, playing the harp and the ukulele, writing a memoir, working on website-building skills, and taking occasional interesting trips. I love to write, and my dream has been to publish at least one personally important book before I die. I hope I can do that in some way. Especially in the beginning, I questioned my ability to go on living without Dennis. This might sound strange, but my cat has kept me alive. He is a beautiful, affectionate, intelligent cat that Dennis picked out and loved deeply. So he was Dennis's cat, and represents him in some way. He needs me, so I continue on.

I'm not as independent as I thought I was. I found someone who is helping me to build in my forest, which is very difficult to do all alone. Recently I read a book entitled *The Widow Down by the Brook*, by Mary MacNeill, a memoir by a widow whose husband died just before he finished building a house in the woods for her. The memoir tells the story of how she learned to become self-reliant. She came to rely on the help of friends and neighbors to finish the house. She continued to live there for many years and became an important part of the rural community. Perhaps the answer for the rest of us is community. You really aren't an island all to yourself; you learn to do more things, but you also develop a network of friends, and learn how to get things done with others. I have to admit that I'm still figuring it all out myself. But I hope that some of the lessons that I have learned will help others who are also learning to survive this most wrenching experience.

Some time ago, as I was sitting in my back yard just before a rainstorm, I experienced a grief attack more powerful than any I had experienced in a couple of years. I hadn't actually cried in a long time. I was remembering how warm and caring Dennis was, and how I miss that, and how musical he was, and how adventurous, and so many other things about him. More and more I find that I look back with a feeling of gratitude that I was able to be with him, the love of my life, for so many years. More and more I feel gratitude replacing the feeling of loss, and that feels like a gift. I hope that you all will find gifts too, that you will find your way towards replacing feelings of loss with gratitude, and sorrow with love, peace, and joy.

John writes:
WARNING!

The following sequence of events occurred after I found my wife Nancy dead on the bedroom floor in our home. The following graphic descriptions and details may cause some to

re-experience unwanted memories. Skip this section if you
wish to avoid potential flashbacks. The facts are presented to
the best of my knowledge and recollection.

"You've reached 911. What is the nature of your emergency?"

"I just walked into the bedroom. My wife rolled off the bed.
She's not responding. She's not moving. She's not waking up.
She doesn't seem to be breathing. I think she might be dead.
Please send help immediately."

*"Sir, can you tell if she's breathing? Do you see her chest
rising and falling? Is she moving?"*

"Why are you asking such stupid questions and wasting
valuable time? I already told you she's not breathing. I can't
tell if her chest is rising or falling. She's unconscious and
unresponsive. She's making no sounds. She's not moving. I
can't move her. Hurry, get some help here right away."

*"Sir, help is on the way. I need you to calm down and stay on
the phone with me. You'll need to go to the door and let them
in when they arrive."*

It seemed like it was taking hours for help to arrive after I
called 911. Really only a few moments passed. But my Nancy
was not moving, breathing, or responding to my feeble
attempts to revive her. I kept saying "wake up, wake up!" My
prompts were to no avail.

Initially three police units arrived. (All city police officers were
trained First Responders.) Emergency Medical Technicians
(EMTs) and the Fire Marshall promptly followed. They cleared
an area to commence cardiopulmonary resuscitation (CPR).
The EMTs contacted and remained in touch with the hospital's
Emergency Room (ER) physician. They hooked up and
armed the defibrillator, started intravenous solutions (IVs), and
attempted to intubate her. One of the EMTs said, "Her jaws

are clenched shut and we cannot intubate her to open an airway". As they prepared to shock her with the paddles, the defibrillator's cold, monotone robotic voice commanded, "Don't shock".

Finally one of the EMTs announced, "We need to transport her to the hospital stat because the blood has pooled in her cheeks." Then, I realized my beloved Nancy was dead at age 61. I had instantly become a widowed survivor. After almost 35 years of marriage, my life immediately changed forever.

Recalling the sequence of events still steals my breath as I recall that fateful day with crystal clarity. Father (Fr.) Anthony, our pastor, and Cindy, the parish nurse, rushed to our house as soon as I notified the parish office. They accompanied me from home to the hospital.

At the hospital the doctor met us. With an objective, clinical coldness he announced, *"I'm sorry she didn't make it."* Fr. Anthony and Cindy went with me into the room, where her body was. Fr. Anthony led the prayers for the dead and anointed her with holy oils. They left. I stayed for a few more minutes and left. There was nothing more I could do for my beloved Nancy. I never expected our marriage to end this way.

Fr. Anthony met me back at the house. He invited me to spend a couple of days at his place. He said he didn't want me to be alone. I politely declined his kind invitation. I had things to do, people to call, and a funeral to plan. I also had to figure out how I was going to tell my 92-year-old mother-in-law her daughter died. What heavy burdens!

The next morning, Fr. Anthony met me at the funeral home. We completed the arrangements, planned the funeral service, and finalized other details. He said he worried about me all night, concerned I might harm myself. I said, "Thanks, but here I am."

For over 30 years, death has mercilessly stalked my family, claiming my spouse, two adult children, five unborn babies, parents, relatives, and friends. In Vietnam I lost comrades-in-arms and observed countless casualties. During my career as a hospital administrator, I observed patients die from many causes. I have seen death close up. (See discussion in Chapter 1.2 "Sudden Loss vs. Lingering Illness".)

Death of anyone close is upsetting, painful, and sad. But nothing remotely compares to the sadness, pain, confusion, and havoc created by the death of a spouse. Losing one's spouse is a world-ending heart breaker, a bitter pill to swallow. Some widowed survivors never recover, withdrawing to a state of perpetual mourning. Some try to reinvent a new life. Others endeavor to plod along as if nothing ever happened. Some retreat to a state of shutdown. The blackout may be temporary but has the potential to become permanent for some widowed survivors.

Each survivor's tale is different. Every story harbors its individual crescendos. My tale of woe is both similar to and uniquely different from others. Each widowed survivor's saga encompasses distinctively different twists, events, memories, and contributing circumstances. Commonly, most widowed survivors' personal experiences reflect shock, pain, sadness, and hurt. Some widowed survivors mourn privately; some openly share their grief and tell their story; and others remain in solitude and bitter denial.

The death rattle intones the same dull timbre each time it blitzes unsuspecting victims. Death ruthlessly leaves survivors holding the proverbial "bag". No one knows the particulars of when, where, how, or why death may strike. Death terminates the life of all living creatures and leaves incomparable anguish in its wake. No one is exempt!

The fallout death causes may differ in marriages that lacked a love connection. In some of these unions, intimacy neither grew nor matured. The partners held no mutual personal respect or regard for each other. The emotional impact, resulting from the death of a spouse in these types of marital unions, may not be as devastating as in a relationship where love, affection, and intimacy flourished. The differences are important and overtly obvious.

There are contrasts, comparisons, and commonalities in many married couples' life and death situations. But the uniqueness of relational interactions and dynamics will inevitably cause variations. Do not be too quick to judge or draw conclusions about the quality of others' relationships. No one knows for certain what occurs in the privacy of another's home.

In May 1977, I moved out of town to begin a new job. (My family dubbed the occasion as the day "John ran away from home".) I was single and not entangled in a long-term relationship. I secretly hoped to meet a "special" someone within the next twelve months; but the prospect seemed unlikely. If I failed to meet a potential significant other, I considered entering the seminary.

Nancy and I met at a Halloween party on the last Friday in October 1977. She was costumed as Dorothy from the Wizard of Oz. Our initial encounter was love at first sight. We belonged to the same singles group, but we had never met nor previously spoken.

The next weekend, we began dating exclusively and became a couple for the next 35 years. Every weekend, after work, I drove "home" on Friday night and returned to work on Sunday evening. (The drive was a 200 mile round trip.) Friends termed our weekends "marathon dates" because we were constantly together. (The winter of 1977-78 was one of the worst southwest Ohio had experienced in many years. Yet, we only missed one weekend.) We spoke by phone every night. Long distance phone bills were horrendously expensive.

We were officially engaged over the second weekend of January 1978. We married the following August. During our marriage, we resided in several states. We celebrated some wonderful highs, enjoyed some exceptional adventures, and suffered some devastating setbacks. Losing all of our children was the most difficult. Such calamities might have ended some marriages. We faced the tragedies and remained together; there was never any doubt in our minds.

Nancy was my "everything": soul mate, lover, best friend, guide, anchor, energy, and reason for getting up every morning. I miss her unconditional love, soothing touch, companionship, humor, balance, support, understanding, peacefulness, perspective, encouragement, and common sense. No relationship is perfect, but we enjoyed and loved each other very much. Our time passed too quickly, literally in the blink of an eye.

1.2 Sudden Loss vs. Lingering Illness

Kathy writes:

When I first started participating in grief support groups, I noticed some differences between the stories of those whose spouse had died suddenly, with little or no warning, and the stories of those whose spouse died from an illness that took months or years. I still don't know which experience is more painful. In the case of sudden loss, the surviving spouse must deal with feelings of shock, unpreparedness, and unfinished business. In the case of lingering illness, the surviving spouse must deal with watching the loved one slowly slip away, the hard work of caregiving, and perhaps discomfort and pain over a long time period.

At one point, I signed up with one grief support group that was sponsored by a hospice organization. As a result, all the other participants were survivors of a loved one's lingering illness that had culminated in hospice care. Eventually I noticed that I was the only one whose spouse had died suddenly. I had many common experiences with others in the group, but I found myself alone whenever I described the suddenness of my loss and my experiences around that. I told the group that I had not had time to say goodbye, but they all said that they had not had time to say goodbye either. They said that one is never prepared for the death itself, even when it has been predicted in advance. These comments are all probably true, but I still feel that there are some differences in the experiences, although they are likely a matter of degree, not absolute differences. Later I discovered the benefit of talking with others who, like me, had experienced a sudden loss. I felt less alone.

For me, there had been no warning, no illness leading up to Dennis's death. He seemed healthy and vibrant. One Friday, he had taken a very long bicycle trip. Then that evening, we both went to one of our favorite places, a bookstore, where each of us bought a book. At home, we sat down at the kitchen table and each of us talked excitedly about our new book. He said that he wanted to read my book when I was done with it. He said that he wanted to take an even longer bicycle trip soon. He talked about a chapter in his book on healthy foods to eat as we age.

That is all I remember before I was awakened at 2:30 AM by the sound of irregularities in his breathing. I tried to awaken him but could not. I called 911 and tried to resuscitate him. The emergency technicians arrived and took him to the hospital, and told me to drive there. Some kind person returned and asked if I was OK to drive myself, and I answered yes. I sat in the emergency room for only a few minutes when someone asked me to come into a private room. There they told me Dennis had died.

The hospital people told me to call someone. I had no idea whom to call, and I didn't want to disturb anyone at such a late hour. But the hospital people kept insisting that I call someone. I called Dennis's sister, who said, "We will be right there". She and her husband came, sat with me, helped me make some immediate decisions, and made sure that I got home OK. I am grateful to them.

My youngest brother came and stayed in my house for a few days. I am grateful to him. That first night, I hardly slept at all and was in complete shock, shaking all night long.

Dennis's death was incredibly sudden. One minute my husband had been there, and the next minute he was gone. I did not have time to say anything meaningful to him, to say goodbye. I did not have time to prepare for what I needed to do next.

That sense of shock lasted a long time, and sometimes there were events that triggered a flashback episode. One time, nearly a year later, close to the anniversary of his death, when I was watching a movie, there was a scene in which a woman was trying fruitlessly to resuscitate a man on an aircraft. I could not stand to watch any more, and had to leave the movie.

I found myself talking to my husband, either at the funeral home or in my own house, to say all those things I would have said if I had known he would die. I found that to be very therapeutic. And I found it helpful to talk to others who had also experienced sudden loss. I found it necessary to allow myself to experience the grief, and the shock, so that I could release it. Maybe these suggestions will benefit those who have experienced sudden loss.

A few years before, my parents had died from lingering illnesses that required hospice care, and I was their main caregiver besides the nursing home. So I have some first-hand experience with lingering loss over time, although the death of a parent is very different from the death of a spouse. I found myself grieving <u>before</u> they died, which surprised me. And it was very difficult to go through all the emergency hospital visits, and witness all their physical difficulties. Maybe participation in a caregiver support group would have helped me at that time. When death came, I felt much emotion, but it wasn't the degree of shock that I felt when my husband died so suddenly. With my parents, I had time to reconcile any unresolved issues. That was very satisfying. We sang together, held hands, and cried together. We had already worked out funeral arrangements. The practical issues were mostly already planned.

Those who experience loss from lingering illness might find help from the hospice organization. Those organizations often provide support for the caregiver, not just for the dying person. Support can begin during the period of illness, a time of great stress. The hospice organization can provide counseling, emotional support, training on how to help the one who is dying, and grief support after the death. And talking with others who are caregivers, and who have experienced a similar type of loss, may reduce the sense of feeling so alone.

John writes:

Death is a ruthless, unscrupulous, devious taskmaster no one can ignore. Death sows misery, confusion, and grueling pain in its throes. Causes of death, as recorded on official documents, feebly compare to the resulting torments inflicted upon survivors. Death of a spouse catapults the widowed survivor to the grief journey's Port of Entry.

Deaths occur in many ways. Some are sudden, while others result from long-term illnesses. Many of the stories, events, situations, and circumstances we read or hear about in the daily news describe deaths from pandemics, terrorism, vehicular accidents, criminal acts, illnesses, or natural disasters.

Learning of the death of a spouse is cataclysmic, the worst news anyone can ever receive. Normal reactions to death trigger regret, remorse, sadness, bewildering shock, and disorientation.

Plausible deniability and disbelief -- "No, it cannot be true!" -- rank among the most common responses. Unexpected death produces surprise, dysfunction, astonishment, and shock. There was no way to prepare. The survivor is literally "caught off guard". Grief sets in when the shock begins to dissipate. The onset of grief may be unabated, disabling, and ongoing.

In my case, death struck swiftly and viciously, snuffing out the candle of our marriage. As reported in Chapter 1.1: "Our Stories", Nancy went to take a nap and I found her dead a couple of hours later. She had rolled off the bed, onto some pillows and quilts, and landed on the floor. She died suddenly and unexpectedly. I felt stunned, betrayed, blind-sided, sucker punched, and beaten with a club. A few hours earlier, we had been discussing spring and summer vacation plans. I know the angels received her and escorted her to heaven. She did not die alone.

The shock kindled my mood swings, which ranged from rage to resignation. My heart was broken. **"How can this be?" "Am I in the midst of a nightmare?" "When do I awaken from this terror?" "When does it end?"** The sinister conclusion was, **"No, it's real, you are awake, and welcome to your new reality."**

The heartbreak of sudden death eradicates all chances to say goodbye. One's beloved is brutally ripped away, here one minute and gone the next. Coping and grieving are permeated by anger, shock, and confusion. The scenario is complex and unfathomable. Nancy's sudden death left me in a stupor of disbelief. There was so much I wanted to say. There was so much I had to say. But I can't speak to her now on this earthly plane. I am forever destined to hold my peace. I could never again tell Nancy in person how much I loved her. The opportunities for long, warm, affectionate physical embraces are gone. I cannot apologize for the times I took her for granted or express my sorrow for snide remarks or unsavory comments. FATE slammed the door shut!

Deprived of the ability to say good-bye produced crushing depression, post-traumatic stress syndrome (PTSD), uncertainty, fear, confusion, and a host of other previously mentioned feelings. "What am I going to do now?" The world I knew abruptly ended as death overthrew my peace, tranquility, and future. It was hard to fully comprehend my new reality. I frequently ask myself, reviewing our final days, "Should I have paid more attention to her physical condition and possible symptomology? Was there something I missed?"

Nothing seemed unusual. We had enjoyed a wonderful weekend prior to the day she died. **"Could I have prevented her death?"** I ask this question over and over again. Answer, **"NO."**

There was a mountain of work, unfinished business, and lists of endless tasks she handled (which I never bothered to learn about in detail) requiring completion. Suddenly all of the lingering chores and tasks seemed to be clamoring for attention and demanding immediate remedy. My most painful and pressing project was planning the funeral, which became a major first step in moving ahead. I also had a rendezvous with a "travel agent" (myself) to book my guilt trip, family and friends to notify, and a beyond overflowing job jar. In one earth-shattering moment my life crashed. In a way, the aftermath of Nancy's death became all about me and the pieces I had to pick up.

I have spoken with several widowed survivors whose spouses died after suffering from a prolonged illness. Perhaps, witnessing the slow eviscerating devastation and life-sapping prowess of a long-term destructive disease process, while hurtful, helped better prepare these survivors for the eventual death of their beloved. Many have reported feeling bamboozled at being unable to alleviate their beloved's suffering and misery. Some claimed they were relieved when death occurred and they express guilt for feeling a sense of relief. Others said they were numb. These survivors watched their beloved wither away and die a little bit each day. Their beloved's dying process lasted days, months, even years. They lived with the dread, terror, and anticipation of knowing the inevitable, inescapable final outcome, but not the exact time. Death tormented them with extended and unmistakable cruelty and pain before claiming their beloved. They resented having to "attend" the dying process. They regretted being unable to alter the final outcome.

One survivor articulated, "I didn't want to lose him, but I wanted his suffering to stop. I wanted his pain to end, not his life. Was I being selfish? I'm forever haunted by those thoughts. Can I ever forgive myself? Will God ever forgive me? Can I forgive God?"

Sudden death and death resulting from prolonged illness create disruption and disheartening remorse. Regardless of the circumstances of death, survivors generally reported experiencing shock, anger, numbness, general sadness, regret, and pain.

Death of a spouse leaves a widowed survivor behind, produces emotional upheaval, and alters the future. Coping and grieving processes are blunted, complex, and unfathomable because so many phenomena collide at the same time.

1.3 Physical and Emotional Sensations

Kathy writes:

The death of a spouse is the most intense physical and
emotional experience that one might ever experience in a
lifetime. Until one experiences it for oneself, one cannot really
understand.

When my husband died, it happened so suddenly that I
experienced symptoms of emotional shock. For the first
several hours, I somehow functioned, with the help of others.
But that night when I went to bed, I shivered all night long, and
slept no more than an hour. Symptoms of emotional shock
vary by individual, but can include shivering, alternating cold
chills and feelings of heat, numbness, an urge to flee,
confusion, sadness, fear, and guilt. Shock can also result in
eating disturbances, sleep disturbances, low energy, pain,
illnesses, memory lapses, decreased ability to concentrate,
and feeling distracted. Symptoms may be delayed by months
and even years, but still be connected to the event.
Symptoms can include nightmares, vigilance, and events that
trigger memories and emotions.

To accept our physical and emotional sensations, no matter
what they are, is important. Feelings of fear, guilt, loss,
sadness, or anger are normal. Don't judge yourself harshly. I
felt tremendous guilt at not saving my husband's life. But I felt
less alone when I discovered that many other widows and
widowers had similar feelings. I also found relief when a
physician who had previously worked in an emergency room
told me that I could not have saved his life without a
defibrillator in my house. But even then, I would still feel guilt.
I find that I must accept my feelings of guilt, allow myself to
feel them, and then release them and let them go.

In the beginning, I cried a lot. I cried every day. I found myself even crying in public, while walking on trails at the nature center where my husband and I used to hike. I had to let myself cry, and not to be embarrassed that someone might see me.

"How long will this last?" That was my question to another widow who had gone through this some years ago, when my experience was still so fresh and painful. I did not know if I could bear to go on like this for very long. "Six months" was her answer. I have heard other widows say that it never goes away. I think the truth is that the loss is always there, but the intensity of the feelings decrease over time. The loss is there, but I have learned new ways to cope with it. The length of time is an individual thing that no one else can dictate. You are the owner of your own grief process, and no one else has the right to tell you how to grieve or when to stop. But I think it might help new grievers to know that the intensity will subside, that there is hope, and that joy will still be possible.

Most widows and widowers I know experience situations and events that trigger memories of the death, or even memories of good times that are reminders of happy days that are gone. I have found that I have become less sensitive to painful triggers of the traumatic event with the passage of time. Before I watch a movie, I still try to read the plot synopsis, so that I can avoid any triggers, or so that I will not be surprised. During my early grieving period, I would cry when I heard a special song we both loved. I might still cry occasionally now, but mostly I enjoy the music and the memory.

Holidays, birthdays, wedding anniversaries, and the anniversary of the death can also be triggers. Sometimes participants in grief support groups let each other know when such an anniversary is coming up, so that others can offer support. Sometimes the grieving survivor can release some of the intense feelings by staying at home to meditate, pray, or

write. Other times the survivor can find relief by spending time
with a close understanding friend.

Be kind to yourself, by taking time to do what you enjoy. An
artist friend who had lost his wife told me that he found solace
by allowing himself to paint. I have been making more time to
write creatively, and to play a musical instrument. Physical
exercise can enhance the mood. Connecting with pets can be
very healing. Now could be a good time to rediscover
activities from the past that you would like to do again.

Slow, deep breathing can bring relief from trauma symptoms.
Start by sitting or lying in a totally relaxed state. Gently and
slowly inhale, filling your belly first, and then your chest. Then
gently and slowly exhale, pulling in your stomach and then
allowing your chest to collapse. But if the sequence becomes
too complicated, don't worry about it, and just breathe
naturally, but slowly and deeply. In a few minutes, you should
feel much calmer.

Widows and widowers are more vulnerable to illness. Before
Dennis's death, I rarely became sick, but afterwards I
experienced several more illnesses than normal. Getting
enough sleep, exercise, and healthy food is more even critical
during this time of vulnerability. An annual complete physical
exam, including a blood test, can be informative. Be careful
about antidepressants, which can have side effects.
Alternatives such as massage, acupuncture, yoga, and herbs
can be effective.

In the beginning, it can be difficult to eat properly. Eating by
myself was one of the most difficult things I had to do in the
beginning. I lost several pounds in a short time. I had to find
new friends with whom to dine. Meetup groups and
widow/widower support groups can be valuable leads for
finding new friends. Refer to the "Resources" section at the
end of this book for a description of Meetup groups and
support groups, and how to access these groups.

John writes:

The death of a spouse abruptly shatters the widowed survivors' routine, sense of balance, and day-to-day life. Survival quickly becomes complex, clouded, confusing, and dubious. Physical and emotional sensations include ideas, memories, images, and feelings. How these reactions manifest themselves defies logic and reason. No scientific model can predict when they will emerge.

A non-widowed spectator may be stunned to observe a survivor simultaneously laughing and sobbing while recounting a story or anecdote about their lost love. Widowed survivors can relive sad and fond memories in the same moment. They may vacillate between rage and resignation. Sadness and relief frequently surface together. Sadness emerges, because one's spouse died; and, relief because the deceased is freed from pain and suffering.

Witnessing this type of event may appear abnormal, bizarre, and insane. But such a display represents a normal expression of emotions for the aggrieved survivor. Post-mortem emotional expressions occur randomly and just happen. The widowed survivor may be a spiritual, mental, physical, and emotional wreck. A non-widowed family member or friend helps best by being present, patient, empathetic, and compassionate. A supportive, reassuring hug is also very helpful and usually welcome. Nothing else needs to be said or done.

Survivors experience guilt if they believe their prayers for their mate's pain to end, resulted in the death. (See Chapter 1.2: "Sudden Loss vs. Lingering Illness".) This awareness creates conflict between emotional health and personal spiritual beliefs. Widowed survivors tend to be self-unforgiving and self-deprecating. They react by punishing themselves.

Grief, mourning, and bereavement disrupt widowed survivors' spiritual, physical, mental, and emotional harmony. (I believe the human psyche consists of these four elements or dimensions.) The delicate sense of balance between human understanding and rationality teeters as the interpersonal disruption and upheaval, attributed to the death of a spouse, knocks the wind out of survivors' sails. The disruption speedily ushers survivors to the brink of unknown, dark domains of uncertainty, confusion, guilt, and regret.

Physical and emotional sensations comprise a dichotomous double-edged sword. Widowed survivors may try to convince themselves that each sensation they experience constitutes an outlier from accepted social customs, norms, mores, or standards. For example, some may believe they are the only ones afflicted by sadness, loneliness, and other tortuous manifestations. So, not wanting to be perceived as a complainer, they mask their feelings and move ahead, frequently to the detriment of their personal well-being.

When one boards the grief journey rollercoaster, the ride heads to points unknown. Detours and bumps, tosses and turns occur unexpectedly and without warning. Hearing a favorite song, visiting a special place, viewing a special landscape, whiffing a special scent, or having a conversation may trigger spontaneous "side trips".

Survivors may experience, exhibit, and complain of pains, symptoms, and ailments including, but not limited to:
- fatigue, lack of ambition, crying, sobbing, weeping uncontrollably;
- bursts of energy, poor motivation, or lack of incentive;
- headaches, restlessness, absent mindedness,
- gastrointestinal maladies, nausea, diarrhea, reduced appetite, sudden weight gain or loss, stomach pain;
- indifference, memory loss, PTSD, nightmares, forgetfulness;

- engaging in addictive behaviors or abuse of alcohol, drugs or other substances;
- shortness of breath, hypertension, lethargy, cardiac palpations, chest pain; and,
- interrupted sleep, insomnia, long term sleep, anger, daytime somnolence, sleep walking, and searching for the deceased – just to name a few.

Upon examination, physicians and health care providers may classify these "maladies" as normal reactions to stress and grief. A widowed survivor, who suffers any of these afflictions, is not alone. Widowed survivors are not neurotic, demented, or mentally incapacitated. Their symptoms are real and may even be indicative of some form of depression.

I once advised a newly widowed friend, "Cry if you want; it's ok. If you're angered by others' remarks and comments, bring it to their attention. But be gentle; remember, people are only trying to help." Many bereaved survivors complain about others' seemingly thoughtless, careless, aggravating, ignorant remarks, and comments. (This matter is covered further in Chapter 4.7: "Coping with Those Who Say or Do the Wrong Thing".)

The terms *grief, mourning*, and *bereavement* are used interchangeably in this book. Mourning and bereavement fall under the main, broad general category of grief. Bereavement and mourning are different aspects of grief. These terms describe the human response to losses caused by death and they symbolize suffering, sorrow, and distress. Death of a spouse constitutes a proper frame of reference for this discussion.

Grief is universal, ageless, and transcends all cultures. History proves:

1. Grief is individual, programmed, lifelong, and unplanned.

2. Grief is neither prescribed nor structured.

3. Grief has no expiration date, shelf life, or barcode. Grief takes as long as one needs it to take. Grief is illogical, pernicious, and unpredictable.

4. Survivors have the right to grieve in accordance with their personal beliefs, values, and traditions.

5. Grief causes physical, mental, emotional, and spiritual havoc.

Grieving is tough work. Grief depletes individual energy, initiative, self-worth, drive, and willingness to care about anything. The bereaved may need an outlet to express their pain to purge their rage. Such sources may be other people, activities, or professional counseling. Anger, rage, crying, and yelling are normal reactions to expressing grief.

Grief is not controllable or dismissible. Grief claims and attaches itself to each survivor in its own form, at its own time, at its own pace, and its own manner. Grief strikes each victim differently. Survivors feel it, experience it, resist it, live with it, or deny it. Grief attacks with a determined, relentless vehemence. Grief, mourning, and bereavement embody a malicious and sobering reality, which takes a long time to resolve. Ultimately, with the passage of time, the pains of grief may abate. The survivor neither fully recovers nor forgets their beloved. But survivors many find the strength and courage to move along their life journey as time progresses and the pains become duller, as they hone and improve their coping skills.

Many survivors reinvent themselves by embracing new adventures. Each set of activities represents a healthy commitment because each survivor chooses to take more control of their future. For many, the intensity of grief subsides with the passage of time.

Part 2. Ceremonies and Tasks

Part 2 describes the ceremonies and tasks that are thrust upon the grieving survivor during the initial period after the loss -- the funeral or memorial service, the writing of an obituary, notifications to people and businesses, and urgent financial transactions. During this time of shock, when the loss is so fresh, the survivor is likely to find it difficult to carry out these responsibilities in an effective way. Also, the survivor may have no experience in performing these tasks. In these chapters, we provide checklists and suggestions for completing these duties.

2.1 The Funeral / Memorial Service

Kathy writes:

Because my husband died so suddenly, there was very little time to plan funeral arrangements and a service. I had to guess what he might have wanted, based on what I could pull out from my memory, and what I knew about him. I found that it helped to draw upon spiritual practices of meditation or prayer, to ask for and find answers. I had to make these decisions quickly, because there was so little time.

The first decision I had to make was where to take the body from the hospital emergency room. Once that decision was made, I met with the funeral home to make subsequent decisions. I had to decide between cremation and burial, and the container, and the timing, and other related decisions.

I had to decide what kind of service to hold, where and when to hold it, and whether or not there would be a dinner afterwards. I had to determine the people to notify about the service, and then make sure they were notified.

My parents had died only a few years before, and they had lived in the same city near us. I had a satisfactory experience making arrangements with their funeral home, and I had found my parents' memorial services very healing. So I decided to use the same funeral home, and to hold the same kind of service for my husband, in the same location. This made the process much easier for me.

A willingness to accept help at this time can significantly reduce stress. Fortunately, I had other people helping with many of these arrangements. By coincidence, on the day after Dennis's death, my brother and I encountered a member of Dennis's dance troupe while walking through a nature center. He agreed to get the word out to the dance community about the memorial service. My brother helped me write and publish the obituary. Another brother and his wife helped arrange the memorial service and the dinner afterwards. My brothers, their wives, and my nephews and nieces helped clean my house. Friends helped notify other old friends. I am grateful to all of them.

We held two services – a private viewing at the funeral home, for family members only, and a more public memorial service at another location. Each event met different needs. This seemed like the right thing to do, for us.

The viewing was a more emotional and primal experience. The event started with everyone speaking in whispers and walking around separated from each other, and visiting the body in small groups. I am usually very shy, but I felt a strong force move me to speak up. I asked everyone to join together to call upon the spirit who moves through everything, or God, depending on their belief system, to give guidance to Dennis so that he could easily go toward light and peace. In response, the whole group stood up and spontaneously formed a circle, holding hands, and each one spoke in turn in a heartfelt way to ask for light and peace for Dennis. This was a group with many divergent beliefs, including Christians, Buddhists, pantheists, and those who could not define themselves, so I was concerned about possible conflict. But instead, each spoke with the imagery of their religion or belief system, speaking from the heart, but all essentially saying the same thing. The circle was very loving and incredibly moving. I was quite surprised. The experience was magical. I know that Dennis would have smiled.

The memorial service was held the next day. Many people came to the service, so it was wonderful that our friend was able to notify so many in the dance community. Many told stories about Dennis's warmth, his kindness, his many interests, and his capacity for fun. I am very shy and usually am unable to speak in large gatherings, but I felt compelled to speak. I talked about the vastness of our love. Once again, I asked everyone to call upon the spirit to send Dennis guidance to move towards peace and light. This felt so important to me, especially since he had died so suddenly.

The Tibetan Book of Living and Dying, which I found helped me more than any other book I was reading during this time, describes how to help people who are dying, but it also says that it is possible to help even after death. The book describes specific practices to help the dead, but it says that even simply directing good thoughts toward the dead will benefit them. In the case of a sudden or violent death, performing the practice or the prayer with more heartfelt fervor can bring greater peace to the dead person. I felt that this effect would be magnified if a large group performed it together. That's why I asked for this from the gathering during both services.

In summary, I found these actions to benefit the planning and implementation of the service:
- If possible, find out what the person who has died wanted for his service and disposition of his body, by locating documents or recalling from memory.

- Draw upon spiritual practices to find answers to lingering questions.
- Do what you are comfortable with, what is healing for you.
- Don't be afraid to accept help from others. You need it, and they need to provide it.
- Do something that helps those who are very close to the dead to grieve, and also helps those who were not as close. Sometimes this might involve separate events.
- Do something that might help the dead person, even if it is simply sending him/her good wishes, or thinking good thoughts.

I think we don't really know with certainty if consciousness persists after death until we have experienced it ourselves. If practices to help the dead have an effect, then we can produce real benefits. If not, then we are not doing any harm. I tend to think there is persistence, because of things I experienced which I describe in a later chapter.

John writes:

Death of a spouse ignites an endless list of time sensitive tasks, chores, and functions that may need to be addressed with some degree of promptness, urgency, and priority. (See Chapter 1.2: "Sudden Loss vs. Lingering Illness".)

Why?

Laws, rules and regulations establish firm, inflexible parameters, requirements, and timeframes. Red-tape bureaucracy neither permits nor accepts any deviations, exceptions, or excuses. The rule of law mandates "comply or else…"

Consider the following logistical checklist for planning a funeral or memorial service. The matter can be a very simple task or sprout into a major, expensive, and complicated project.

- Do we want a private service for family and friends or a public event?
- Will remains be embalmed, cremated, or donated to science?
- How will we clothe our beloved?
- Do we want to display photos, videos, or storyboards memorializing their life? Film the service or not? Publication of memorial cards, memorial books, and obituary? Brochures must be selected and ordered.
- Select burial container: casket, urn, or something else?
- Visitation plans must include calling hours.
- Open or closed casket? Can the deceased's body be shown? Should the deceased be photographed in the casket?
- Consider service schedule and availability of the church, temple, funeral home, or gravesite.
- Are clergy and facility staff available? What is the plan for prayers, type of service, music, pallbearers?
- Will final disposition of the body be burial or placement in a mausoleum? Will cremains be placed in a columbarium, taken home, sprinkled, or buried?
- What were the loved one's final wishes regarding the funeral? Did they leave documented final plans, wishes, or instructions?
- If the deceased was a veteran, will there be a military honor guard? Who will notify or contact the military?
- Will we host an after service luncheon or social gathering?

Amazingly, depending on the scope of the event, arrangements can coalesce in as few as 24 hours. Funerals can last from 1 to 8 days. The longer it takes, the more expensive it becomes. Ornate, complicated funerals require intense orchestration and planning. Costs increase proportionately. Is there enough money to cover the costs of the "planned funeral"? How much can we afford? How much do we want to afford? How will potential changes in the original plans be managed? Did the deceased prepay for their funeral?

For those who may anticipate transporting remains across state lines for burial, legal requirements cover everything from preparation of the body, type of transportation container, licenses to transport the body, and coordination with a mortuary at the destination. Considerations include costs, facilities, cemetery preparations, and accommodating family and others who may wish to attend. Dealing with reputable funeral providers simplifies planning and logistics.

Stress and feeling rushed are nerve wrecking, but there is a sense of urgency. The bereaved spouse can realize some relief by allowing others to help. For a sole surviving spouse the experience can be akin to planning in a fog. At a time when one is most vulnerable, distraught, mentally stressed, and not thinking clearly, an incompetent or unscrupulous service provider can create pandemonium.

The time immediately after the death of a spouse can pose the worst possible scenario for funeral planning. The widowed survivor is driven by expressions of love, wanting to do "what's right because it's right" by their loved one, and have a feeling of being pleased with their decisions. Maintaining delicate equilibria can be emotionally exhausting, financially draining, frustrating, confusing, and dispiriting. For these reasons, as stated earlier, relying on the support and input of family members and trusted friends can prove to be most beneficial.

Circumstances may dictate the availability of family, especially out-of-towners' ability to attend. What needs and arrangements have surfaced for their reception, lodging, and hospitality? (See Chapter 2.3: "Notifying People and Businesses".)

Do religious traditions, cultural customs, or other rituals need to be observed?

There are choices about appropriate attire for the funeral. American culture and custom generally accepts wearing dark foreboding colors or black. In some circles, to dress otherwise is considered gauche, out of line, or unfathomable. Black usually denotes mourning and bereavement. Black reflects the gloominess of the situation and the potential "dark" times ahead for the survivor. Widowed survivors understand the lighted candle, representing their lives together, has been extinguished. Time becomes obscure.

Contemporary thought and accepted social practices endorse celebrating the life of the deceased. A celebration of life theme permits mourners to wear colorful clothing and pay a happy final tribute to the deceased. This change of attitude is a stark contrast to wearing the traditionally accepted dark, drab colors. Many choose to celebrate the life of the deceased and avoid wearing the customary black. Sometimes mourners are invited to attend a social gathering after the funeral. Increasingly, post-funeral service events, gatherings, receptions, or luncheons celebrate the deceased's life.

Anyone who has witnessed a funeral in New Orleans' French Quarter may have observed the deceased is borne to their final resting place in a parade. The band plays funeral dirges, festive marches, and celebratory music. Mourners, clad in colorful and festive clothes, sing, sashay, and dance their way to the cemetery.

2.2 The Obituary

Kathy writes:

Writing an obituary isn't mandatory, but such a document notifies people who might not otherwise know of the death, and provides information for attending the funeral, memorial service, or viewing. First identify where you wish to publish the obituary, and then look at examples of some that have already been published. I wrote both a short version for the newspaper and a longer version for the alumni magazine.

The obituary normally includes the following, at minimum:
- The full name of the person who has died
- Date of death
- Age at death
- City and state where death occurred
- Names of those left behind, including spouse, parents, siblings
- Names of spouses of siblings can also be included. Often first names of spouses of siblings appear in parentheses after full sibling names.
- Date, time, address, and phone number for any service or event open to the public
- Where any memorial contributions can be sent, including organization name, address, and phone number.

The longer version of the obituary includes the items above, and also biographical information, and can include a photograph.

I found writing the longer biographical version to be a satisfying and healing process, because it caused me to reflect on my husband's fine qualities and amazing accomplishments, and allowed me to craft a statement that would help memorialize his achievements in public view. Obituaries are available to be read by many people, and can appear on the web for a very long time.

This is another case in which you can ask for help if you need it. Sometimes funeral homes can provide help. Family and friends may help provide memories. My brother proofread my documents and helped me to distribute them. You need not produce the obituary all by yourself, unless you want to.

John writes:

An obituary is a notice announcing the death of a person. An obituary, shared or published in the public media, minimally mentions the deceased's name, birth and death dates, details or circumstances of the death, family connections, and service arrangements. Composing the obituary is strictly a matter of subjective, personal preference.

Some obituaries are beautifully written literary pieces depicting the life history of the deceased in amazing detail, a mini biographical sketch. A photo of the departed may grace some obituaries. The obituary becomes part of the final tribute paid to the deceased and presents a summary of their life story.

Preparing an obituary places additional pressure on the funeral planner. The obituary author can continuously question, "Did I say the right thing?" "Did I omit something significant?" "Did I say enough?"

Some individuals write their own obituary before they die. Others have obituaries written by survivors. Some choose to have no obituary.

From my personal experience, obituaries are a matter of individual preference and discretion. Newspaper classified advertising department personnel realize obituaries occupy column space and produce revenue and they charge accordingly. An obituary may add to overall funeral expenses.

Someone asked me if there were specified standards that determine what constitutes a good obituary. There are none of which I am aware. The only standard format might be a newspaper's template or a reference in a book.

Some families prefer a short announcement with salient facts. Others publish a written tribute worthy of publication as a news article. Style, length, and content rest with the discretion of the survivors or the deceased's final wishes and publication requirements. Some obituaries are posted on social media sites.

2.3 Notifying People and Businesses

Kathy writes:

After Dennis died, one of the first things I did was to make a list of people and businesses to notify about his death. The first people to notify were those who needed to know soon because they might attend the service. This can be difficult when the death is so new, and takes time. If there are others in the family or close friends who know these other people, it's good to allow them to help by contacting the others. I made a list and checked off names as they were notified. I did forget some people who found out later, and that can be difficult. But this is an incredibly wrenching time, very likely unprecedented in your whole life, and you must forgive yourself any lapses at a time like this, even if others are offended. They should understand and forgive, but more importantly, you must forgive yourself.

So I made a list of friends, relatives, and close associates at work. I tried to determine any appointments Dennis had, and contacted those people.

Later, after the memorial service, after everyone had gone home, I contacted businesses that needed to be notified. Here is a checklist that might be helpful:
- Employer, if spouse had been working, to inquire about benefits, including life insurance
- Social Security Administration, to notify of death and determine your eligibility for death benefits
- Veterans Administration, if spouse had been receiving benefits, or if you might be eligible
- Provider of spouse's pensions
- Provider of your pensions
- Health insurance, to notify of change in coverage
- Auto insurance, to notify of change in coverage

- State department of motor vehicles, to cancel driver's license
- County courthouse, to switch vehicle title to your name, if applicable
- Spouse's physicians
- 401K and/or IRA custodian, inheritor services group
- Banks and credit unions, to remove spouse's name from joint accounts, and to find out process for inheriting spouse's individual accounts
- Credit card companies, to close accounts
- Subscriptions, memberships, or regular shipments that are no longer needed

Some sources also recommend notifying the three credit reporting agencies -- Equifax, Experian, and TransUnion — to reduce the chance of identity theft. If you do this, instruct the agency to list all accounts as: "Deceased. Do not issue credit." The agencies may require an original death certificate, and proof that you are the surviving spouse or executor. A sample form is available at www.oprm.va.gov/docs/DeathNotificationChecklist.pdf, which also has a checklist similar to the one above. But if you do not notify the credit reporting agencies, it is possible that they will receive notification anyway, from the Social Security list of deceased people.

This checklist is not necessarily a complete list, due to individual circumstances. The funeral home might already have notified some of these organizations, so check with them first. In my case, the funeral home notified the Social Security Administration that my husband had died. But I still contacted the Social Security Administration to find out my own eligibility for death benefits, and to make application. That application does not happen automatically.

Many of these organizations will require a copy of the death certificate, but might not require an original certified certificate. This is an important distinction because there is a charge for each additional original death certificate. A few might require an original certificate, so be sure to request a few extras (at least 5 to 10 certified copies) when ordering them. Usually death certificates are available from the funeral home.

The next chapter discusses financial transactions in more detail.

John writes:

Notifications after the death of a spouse are emotionally draining, de-spiriting, exhausting, mentally arduous, time-sensitive, and mind-boggling. (See Chapter 2.1: "The Funeral/Memorial Service".) A newly widowed survivor may not be in the appropriate frame of mind to make needed notifications. In these cases, they may engage the assistance of relatives and friends to complete the task.

Conclude the task as quickly and diligently as possible. Speak with patience, priority, and urgency. Completing notifications may be very time consuming. Some of the people on the notification list may want to chat about the details of the death.

Categories of notification include, but are not limited to:

1. Immediate family and next-of-kin may want to attend the funeral, send memorials, chat, pay their respects, and lend support. They need time to readjust their schedules and make arrangements. Their participation is kindled by love, respect, family duty, curiosity, gaining a sense of closure, or all of the above. Some family members have been overheard remarking "the only time we get together is weddings and funerals." What does this say about the world in which we live? Other family members may be limited by distance, conflicting schedules, or lack of financial affordability.

2. Friends, neighbors, colleagues, business associates, and acquaintances may be notified for reasons similar to those cited under immediate family. If the deceased was employed, his/her employer must be notified. Complete employer notification hastily because survivor (death) benefits may be available. These benefits may help defray funeral expenses. Employers, which offer benefits, require official copies of death certificates before starting to process any death claims or settlements. Benefit plan administrators cannot merely "take your word for it". Their fiduciary responsibility requires them to verify the death actually occurred. The bureaucracy involved can be cumbersome and lengthy. Financial distributions involved may include life insurance, survivor benefits, retirement funds, and continuation of medical and dental coverages for the surviving family. Prompt notification facilitates beginning the claims process quickly and expedites settlements, payments, and payouts.

3. Social Security, Veterans Administration, and government agencies must be contacted to report the death, stop benefit payments, and begin the process of settling death claims. Government benefits paid after the date of death must be returned or repaid, unless they are covering the previous month before the death. They are classified as overpayments. Prescheduled appointments the deceased may have scheduled must be cancelled. Copies of official death certificates will be needed. I strongly urge each survivor, and/or their helpers, to keep dated, written records of the conversations with agency representatives. Such documentation may be useful in recalling details, dates and times, and names of contact persons at a later time, should the need arise.

4. Debtors, financial institutions, and creditors must be notified to accommodate repayment plans, transfer balances due or owed to the estate's executors or survivors, and clarify who, if anyone, may access savings, checking, or investments accounts, and safe deposit boxes. Authorizations for an individual to access, if one is not named on the account, may require court orders. If the deceased's will is in probate, evidence is required to establish the identity of those authorized to transact business on behalf of the estate. Access to credit cards, bank accounts, and other means utilized by the deceased to transact business may be closed, held in abeyance, or amended until identity of the executor is established. Certified or original copies of death certificates, estate documents, and wills are needed. Keep detailed notes of all contacts and conversations. In my experience, some of the debtors, financial institutions, and creditors returned the death certificate, as they made a copy for their files.

5. Local authorities are usually notified through the funeral home, if one is used. Help from an attorney, executor, trustee, or appointed estate administrator may be needed to plod through, straighten out, and complete legal requirements for death certificates, finalizing public records, cemetery plans, church arrangements, and other related tasks. Titles to property, motor vehicles, and real estate must be updated and amended to reflect current ownership or responsible parties. Insurance documents, financial records, investments, savings accounts, checking accounts, and the like must be identified, processed, and settled. Original or certified copies of death certificates will be needed. Maintain detailed notes.

Notifications must be handled with priority to minimize potential difficulties and delays that could result from procrastination or delays. Timeliness is critical.

Be bold, forward, and unafraid to seek assistance or ask questions of an attorney, CPA, financial advisor, next of kin, or trusted friends. There is no shame in being frustrated, confused, or befuddled when trying to settle an estate. Requesting help is more prudent than making expensive mistakes, especially for a widowed survivor who does not deal with the death of a spouse, or settlement of an estate every day.

2.4 Urgent Transactions

Kathy writes:

Do not rush into any major financial decision, such as selling your house, giving away money, buying an annuity or life insurance, or buying or selling assets in large quantities, for at least a year, and possibly two years, after your spouse has died. If you receive a large lump sum, such as proceeds from life insurance, consider placing it into a money market fund, where it will be liquid, before making further decisions. This is a time of great emotional turmoil, which could result in decisions you regret later. Also, if there is a will being processed through probate court at this time, or property still being distributed, any major financial transaction might complicate matters.

This chapter discusses those financial transactions that must take place now – settling the estate, moving assets to heirs, collecting death benefits, and ensuring cash flow. Other less pressing transactions can be dealt with later.

If your spouse left a will or trust, find the most recent copy and contact the executor. The executor must initiate the process of gathering the assets, paying debts, expenses, and taxes, and distributing the remaining assets to the designated parties, as specified in the will or trust. If you are the executor, you might want to contact an estate attorney for help. This could be the attorney who drafted the will, if that attorney is available.

If your spouse did not leave a will or trust, this is referred to as "intestate". In this case, if there is a large estate, contact an estate attorney for help. There are rules of inheritance that determine who will receive the proceeds of the estate, and these rules vary from state to state. Many types of assets are not included in the estate, such as life insurance proceeds, IRA accounts, pensions, annuities, bank accounts, or credit union accounts, if there is someone specifically named as a beneficiary. Accounts that you held jointly with your spouse are usually not included either. But contact an attorney if you have any question.

If your spouse did not leave a will or trust, and the estate is very small, it is possible that your state will allow heirs to obtain property of the deceased person without going through probate. The state of Kentucky, for example, allows the surviving spouse to go to the courthouse, obtain a document, and present it to the bank where the deceased spouse had an individual account, to obtain those funds. However, this can happen only if the total amount of such accounts does not exceed an amount specified by law. Search the web for the law, or contact an attorney for clarification. Contact the bank to find out what it requires, and contact the courthouse in your county to find out how the requirement can be implemented.

If your late spouse held a credit card in his/her name only, and that credit card has significant rewards, such as a large number of frequent flier miles, contact the credit card company before closing that card, to find out how you might inherit those rewards. You might need to fill out a form, get it notarized, and send it in with a copy of the death certificate. In my case, I had a credit card with the same financial institution, with my own frequent flier miles, and his were added to mine.

Many people do not realize that Social Security can provide survivor's benefits to those younger than 62. Widows and widowers can get reduced survivor benefits as early as age 60, and there are circumstances that provide benefits at younger ages. Widows and widowers can get survivor benefits and later switch to benefits on their own work record as late as age 70. By making a switch past full retirement age, they can earn delayed retirement credits. Or conversely, they can start with their own work record at age 62 and switch to survivor benefits as late as their full retirement age. But which strategy is most beneficial depends on the unique situation.

Make sure that the Social Security office files an application for only <u>one</u> of the two benefits (survivor vs. your own work record)! Otherwise, you might lose the ability to switch to the other benefit later. The Social Security office sometimes files for both benefits simultaneously. You may need to make an explicit statement in writing to "restrict the scope" of the application to survivor benefits, or to your own work record.

Check the Social Security website at <u>www.ssa.gov</u> for the detailed regulations, and check with a financial advisor with knowledge specific to social security for advice that fits your situation. Social Security is not equipped to give advice, but only to explain the regulations. There is now a certification for financial advisors called NSSA (National Social Security Advisors), so you can look for that certification when seeking a financial advisor.

If you have a pension, be sure to contact your own pension provider as well as your spouse's provider. You might be entitled to an increase in your payment, since your pension no longer must cover a beneficiary, depending on the terms of the pension.

If you don't already have a trusted financial advisor, check with family and friends for references, or check with the National Association of Personal Financial Advisors (NAPFA) at <u>www.napfa.org</u>. NAPFA advisors receive compensation based only on fees for advice, and so their advice should not be biased by any motivation to sell stocks or annuities, for example.

There are differences in the way you file income taxes in the year of the death. Contact your tax advisor, if you have one. Or your tax software will guide you through the process with its questions, or the publications on the IRS website (www.irs.gov) will explain. Check also the income tax website for your state.

Set up a system for paying bills. Collect the current bills into a file as they come in. You might need to find your spouse's checkbook to identify what the regular bills are. Make a list of the bills, the amount or average amount, and the date due each month. Check off the list when the bills are paid. This decreases the chances that you will miss any bills. Later you can use this information to put together a budget.

John writes:

Unbridled frenzy reigns after the death of a spouse, and survivors are drafted into planning a funeral. The process may involve multiple and unfamiliar financial transactions and fiscal commitments. Prior to committing to any final agreements, contracts, or papers, read all documents carefully and ask questions before executing and signing them. Optimally, the widowed survivor should be accompanied by family members or friends who may be in a more rational emotional state.

The mortician, funeral director, or county coroner has usually removed the body from the site of where the death occurred. The funeral provider, in possession of the remains, needs to know the family's plans and wishes within a relatively short time, usually within hours of the death.

Initial questions concern the decedent's identity, instructions for preparation and disposal of remains, payment arrangements, and follow up for future meetings, if needed. The event is a well-rehearsed and routine scenario to seasoned professionals.

This situation is neither conducive nor optimal for the newly widowed survivor. "What the heck we're in shock!" Delaying decisions could result in major expenditures, significant long-term financial obligations, and substantial future turmoil.

Take as much time as needed to steady matters; control and understand the pace. Due diligence is of the essence. Avoid the proverbial "rushing into things!" *Tempus fugit* has no standing with regard to financial transactions at this critical, vulnerable time. One may be better off incurring financial penalties or delinquency notices than to make wrong decisions.

As mentioned in Chapter 2.3: "Notifying People and Businesses", widowed survivors benefit from consulting or conferring with family, friends, or trusted advisors when encountering these situations. Fortunately, most funeral service providers and professionals are ethical, scrupulous, compassionate, honest people with excellent reputations, good references, and high degrees of integrity. Dependable, credible providers vastly outnumber those of dubious character.

Do not blindly leap from the precipice! Be careful! Be judicious! Be prudent! Conserve your assets! Do Not Rush. Consequences can be devastating.

Part 3. Initial Adjustment

Part 3 describes the initial adjustment that takes place after the period of the funeral and memorial service, but during the first weeks and months after the loss. These chapters describe practical, financial, and emotional issues, and suggestions for working through these issues. It also describes sources of strength and support that worked for us.

3.1 The Practical Stuff

Kathy writes:

After the visitors were gone, and the most pressing tasks were completed, I needed to continue with everyday life. I started to discover all those things that Dennis had taken care of that I did not know how to do. The transition was especially difficult because he died so unexpectedly, so that there had been no time for him to pass practical information along to me. This was the time for detective work, for finding clues about where he purchased important items, how he maintained household equipment, how he prepared food, what ongoing financial transactions he handled. This was also the time for seeking help from family, friends, or the marketplace.

Dennis was highly skilled at finding the highest quality products at the lowest price, but I did not know where he purchased all the things we used. Fortunately, I was able to discover most sources through his computer bookmarks and his emails. I made a list of the important items that I would need on a regular basis, and the source for each of those items.

I didn't know how to clean the water distiller, or replace the furnace filter, or fix the vacuum cleaner. I started to look through the kitchen drawer that contains manufacturer's manuals, and prepared to call phone numbers marked on the equipment. I found a phone number for the company that maintained our furnace. Eventually a friend came over and helped me to maintain these things.

A kind neighbor appeared at my door and offered to help me rake the autumn leaves. My sister-in-law also helped. Computer hardware experts, who were colleagues at my workplace, helped me gain access to Dennis's laptop so that I could use it. I checked with people I knew and trusted for names of companies that repair, maintain, or perform handy work.

I found Dennis's checkbook, and used it to make a list of bills, along with estimated amount, and date due. I used this as a checklist so that I would not miss any bills. I added a column for actual amount paid. At the end of the year, I adjusted the estimated amounts to match the actual history. Now I had a budget. I added up my monthly income and compared it against the total of my estimated monthly payments. If the estimated payments exceeded my income, I would work on a plan for reducing expenses or increasing income.

Be alert for potential scams that target widows. Watch out for anyone contacting you with fake debts allegedly owed by your late spouse. Do not give out any personal or identifying information (such as birthdate, social security number, or even your name) to anyone you do not know on the phone, even if that person sounds legitimate. Be suspicious of any email that you receive that asks for money, even if you know the owner of the email address. That email account might have been stolen by someone else. Do not click on any links in an email; instead, open a browser and type in the link address. Do not download anything from the Internet unless you have searched for it yourself and know the source is reliable. Review each credit card purchase on your bill to make sure that it is yours, and dispute any that are not. Read articles on the AARP website about scams that target older people, so that you will be informed and prepared.

Adapting to the practical aspects of life without your partner takes time. Be patient with yourself, and reach out to others.

John writes:

"Now my spouse is gone! What am I supposed to do about the bills, day-to-day activities, finances, and living the rest of my life in general?"

Nancy took care of "stuff" during the course of our marriage. We agreed on the division of roles and chores shortly after we married. Subsequently, I did not delve too deeply into the thick of things because I knew she handled matters competently, efficaciously, and carefully. We'd learned early in our marriage that two people could not easily manage one checkbook. With more effort at communication, coordination, and cooperation, we probably could have made it work. But we chose the solution best suited to our needs.

Once we agreed on the need for having one household financial manager, I happily relinquished the responsibility. We never quibbled about "this is my money and that's your money" because it was always "our money". We deposited our paychecks, with no problem, into the same checking account. We established the house fund.

If I ran short of cash, I used a credit or debit card. I usually told her about transactions, if I remembered. When there was an error, I was usually the culprit. Occasional overdraft notices vexed us. We would discuss the matter. She was scrupulously conscientious about our family finances. Nancy was a capable and effective household financial manager. We never incurred late fees, received delinquent notices, or were turned over to collections for failure to pay bills in a timely manner.

Money was available when needed. There was generally no worry. We conferred about major purchases. If a planned purchase was out of range, we postponed the expenditure until we accumulated the required funds.

We were both employed. She went back to work when the children were of school age. As I advanced in my career, we agreed I should establish a personal checking account to fund daily personal, business, and job related expenses since I was doing more traveling.   But Nancy was our primary financial manager.

After retirement, we downsized to one checking account. Life became simpler. We both knew the fiscal state of our union. But she remained the primary day-to-day fund custodian, financial manager, and checking account signatory. When she died, I knew about the state of our checking account, finances, household bills, and expenses that she handled so well. I remembered the basics of checkbook management and paying bills from my bachelor days, or premarital formative years (getting house broken).

3.2 Living Within Your Means

Kathy writes:

The death of a partner is shattering emotionally, but often it can be devastating financially at the same time. A major source of income may be lost. There might not be a life insurance policy. Pensions, when they exist, often provide only 50% of the previous income stream to the beneficiary. Social security allows only one spouse's benefit to continue, although the survivor takes the larger of the two benefits. But many household expenses continue at the same level as before the death. Those expenses are not cut in half.

The survivor might find himself or herself needing to cut back substantially on expenses, and even perhaps having to move to a less expensive location. Some survivors find this move relatively easy, an escape from painful memories of the ending of the loved one's life. But others find it painful, as they are torn away from the familiar place where happy times were shared, at the same time that they are experiencing the pain of the loss of the partner.

I feel lucky that I was not forced to leave my house. I am one who finds comfort in the familiar and in the good memories. But I notice that I would have been financially more comfortable if my husband were alive now.

One strategy to cope with financial issues is to continue working, perhaps longer than previously planned. I could have chosen to stop working when my husband died. Instead, I chose to keep working, partly because stopping work would mean a big change on top of another big change, increasing my stress level. But it wasn't easy to go back to work just after the death of my husband. I compromised by switching to part-time. I continued working until I felt ready to stop. That extra year and a half helped me financially.

I know other widows who continue working into their late 60s. Not only does continued work result in an increased income stream during the remaining work years, but also it can earn delayed retirement credits for social security, and provides opportunity for additional contributions to retirement accounts. Some are able to find satisfaction in their work or in friendships formed there.

But not everyone can work or wants to work past normal retirement age. There are other ways besides working in your previous occupation to gain income. Some people find ways to turn their hobby or passion into income stream. Those who enjoy writing might learn how to create a blog, and then sell advertising or their own products or services on the blog. Or they might write a book. Some might choose to teach online. I know someone who works for a company to market consumer products on the web. There are many possibilities, and many of them can involve working from home, if that is your preference.

Besides new products, there is a market for used products. You might have assets in your house that can be turned into cash. If you learn to sell on an online website such as eBay, you will discover a wider market than you would find at a yard sale or local second-hand store. You would need to learn how to photograph, price, and describe your items, communicate with customers, and ship to them. At the same time, you might be clearing your house of clutter.

Or you might have monetary assets that could become a source of income, now or in the future. Consult with an independent fee-based financial advisor for ideas. Read books on financial topics that interest you, and become more knowledgeable.

Even if you never increase your incoming cash flow, if you decrease unnecessary expenses it will feel as if you gave yourself a raise. Look at your list of monthly bills, with the actual amounts that you have been paying. Examine each line item on that list, and ask yourself if there is any way to decrease the amount. After Dennis died, I called the phone companies and internet provider and asked questions about how I could change my service to minimize my phone bill. I found out how my utility companies charge, and how I could reduce those bills. I started preparing food at home more, and started purchasing food in bulk to reduce the expense in the long term. I started saving coupons.

Sharing housing could reduce expenses significantly, and provide companionship. If you share housing, finding a housemate who is compatible with you is critical. Compatibility is more likely if the potential housemate is a friend that you already know, but be careful that the arrangement does not destroy the friendship. In the beginning, discuss household rules and how you will handle any conflict.

John writes:

Financial management eventually becomes easier to oversee after the death of a spouse, as the widowed survivor becomes better oriented and informed. The survivor must develop a functional system for managing finances. There is no formula, curriculum, or standard outline. Most widowed survivors become competent but never really graduate. If finances remain untended, they can become problematic for the widowed survivor. (See Chapter 2.4: "Urgent Transactions".) Adjustments may be needed in deciding how to live on one income or contemplating when or if to return to work.

Financial management issues, and related matters, initiate a set of pressing conditions urgently baying for attention and resolution. New, perhaps unanticipated, financial challenges can emerge after the death of a spouse. Consider the following list and related questions (Within this framework "I" and "we" may be used interchangeably. If there are children use "we". If the survivor is childless use "I".)

Some questions, warranting consideration, follow. These ideas are posed to help avert calamity and potential insolvency. The list is not all-inclusive.

- Can I (we) afford to do some of the things I (we) used to do?
- What modifications are needed to live within my (our) financial means?
- Can I (we) continue with or maintain my (our) former standard of living?
- Can I (we) keep the house?
- Do I (we) need to move to be closer to family? Thus the challenge becomes, "How do I (we) choose to continue in my (our) new survival mode?"
- From paid death benefits, what do I (we) do with the proceeds? Invest? Save? Repay old debt? Spend?
- What debts occurred as a result of final illness and medical bills, the funeral, burial, etc.? How will these be paid?
- Were there unknown bills or debts?
- Are all bills and debts, of which I am aware, current?
- Is it advisable to meet with or engage the services of a banker, financial planner, tax expert, estate planner, or attorney?

However, once the death of a spouse sinks in, the survivor will readily admit how much they depended on the expertise of their mate. Survivors quickly comprehend they were not as abreast or informed about household financial matters as much as they thought they were.

Sometimes financial disparities can become bottomless pits. Unaddressed, unresolved, or unmanaged financial questions may be indicative of concerns which behoove the survivor to quickly learn about, take control of, and become aware of what really is happening. Promptness, accuracy, and alacrity are vital. Problems may surface, because the financial partner of the marriage died. This conjecture is not meant to imply the deceased partner was withholding financial information about the state of the union. Rather the comment reflects the confidence of the survivor in the deceased's ability to capably manage the household finances.

3.3 The Emotional Stuff

Kathy writes:

Immediately after Dennis's death, I was literally in shock, shaking all night long as I tried to sleep. I used the word "shattered" to try to describe how I felt. I said, "I knew my husband since 1969, and his roots in me ran deep, so I feel that half of me has been ripped out." Never in all my life did I anticipate how severe my emotions would be.

I have heard many other widows describe similar emotions. But I have also heard a few of them say that the pain never ends. If someone had told me in the beginning that what I felt would never end, I think I would have despaired. The truth is that over time feelings change and you are transformed. You don't "get over it"; you don't forget your spouse and your loss, and there is still pain, but you learn to cope with it. And the intensity of the pain lessens over time, so that you can bear to go on living. If your loss is very recent, I feel a powerful obligation to tell you this. There is hope.

The first day after Dennis died, I kept thinking I was in a nightmare and might wake up soon. The next day, I was writing an obituary, and caught myself almost calling to him to ask his father's middle name. There were so many things he used to do that I would have to do now, and so many reminders. His alarm clock still went off in the morning with prompts to change the furnace filters, put tea bags into my briefcase, and other tasks. His new shoes were sitting next to the kitchen table. He had unopened packages. I felt as if he had just left briefly and might return soon. I could not even contemplate donating his clothes – it felt as if he might need them!

In the early weeks, I cried every day. I went to the nature center where we used to walk so often, and I cried all along the trails, and I didn't care if anyone saw me. I cried at my desk at work. I cried when I left the office and walked through the parking lot where I used to call him on my cell phone to tell him I was returning home.

My grief came in waves. Sometimes it was overwhelming, and I didn't know if I could go on. When I went to pick up the ashes at the funeral home, I was completely overcome by seeing such a small box, and by the finality, and I was sobbing and could hardly stand up. The funeral home people sat with me and then offered to deliver the ashes to my house, so I accepted that offer and received the ashes a few days later. By then I was calmer and it felt right that the ashes were with me.

In the first few months, the loneliness was intense, and the silence deafening. I found it difficult to eat by myself, and difficult to return to an empty house. Daily phone calls from my brother and from a friend helped me, and visits to relatives and friends on holidays helped. But in the end, I returned to the empty house.

The first Thanksgiving without him was only three weeks after his death. I visited a family gathering at a farmhouse in Pennsylvania. There I met a friend of my brother, and she was a widow. I asked her how long these intense feelings would last. She predicted, "six months". I wasn't sure that I believed her, but her words gave me hope. She recommended a book by Joan Rivers called *Bouncing Back* (listed in the "Resources" section of this book). Later I read that book, and found that it did offer many positive suggestions.

A year later, I returned to that same farmhouse on Thanksgiving. That same widow was present, and she remarked that I seemed much more centered and calm.

Some months earlier, a close colleague at work had commented on the changes in me. So that widow's prediction turned out to be correct. For me, this demonstrated the changing nature of grief over time, the lessening of intensity, and the process of coping and adapting. I believe that there is hope for every survivor to grow and change, and to find a new life.

After the phase of intense emotions in the beginning, there may be long stretches of time when you don't cry and are calm, but suddenly you might find yourself overcome with strong feelings of grief. I have heard many widows call this a "grief attack". Sometimes the attack might be triggered by an event that reminds you of an experience with your spouse. I mentioned in a previous chapter my reaction to a movie that I watched around the first anniversary of Dennis's death, during a scene in which a woman tried to save the life of a man having a heart attack, but could not. This was such an intense reminder of Dennis's death that I bolted from the room and collapsed, sobbing, on the floor of another room.

In this case, the grief attack reminded me of symptoms of posttraumatic stress disorder (PTSD). PTSD is a reaction to extreme stress or trauma. The symptoms can include flashbacks, recurring dreams about the event, loss of memory of the event, distress when exposed to circumstances associated with the event, avoiding circumstances associated with the event, difficult sleeping, difficulty concentrating, and hypervigilance, that continue for a long time after the event took place. Originally, PTSD was a diagnosis associated with soldiers returning from war, but eventually mental health practitioners noticed that the same symptoms were experienced by others exposed to violently traumatic situations, such as victims of violent crime, survivors of traffic accidents, and witnesses to disasters.

The death of a spouse is trauma, and so feelings of grief can be mixed with those of PTSD. In my case, the death of my husband was a completely unexpected event that occurred suddenly, and came as a complete shock. It happened in the middle of the night while I was sleeping. For months, or longer, I had trouble sleeping, I avoided recalling the actual event, I had difficulty concentrating, and events such as that movie acted as "triggers" putting me right back into the traumatic event, so that I was reliving it.

Several modes of therapy have been developed to help ameliorate the effects of PTSD. Some of these therapeutic techniques might be beneficial for relieving PTSD symptoms for widows. In my case, I have found that the symptoms have faded over time. I have used general grief support therapy, and have not used therapy specific to PTSD. But I find it useful just to understand what I am experiencing, and to know that it is normal.

I have found a sense of connection from participation in widows' and widowers' support groups, by talking with others who understand what I have experienced because they have lived it themselves. I have found healing from talking with a therapist who understands grief. I have found strength from engaging in meditative practices that connect me with spiritual energy. I have found direction by doing creative work each day that moves me closer to my life's purpose.

Guilt is an emotion that appears commonly in the grieving process. To allow yourself to be overwhelmed with thoughts of what you should have done, or the terrible things that you thought you did, and the effects that you thought resulted, is often tempting. Sometimes there is anger or remorse over flaws in the relationship. But human beings are imperfect, and likewise all relationships are imperfect. By their very nature, close relationships involve conflict as well as agreement, estrangement followed by harmony. In time, the memories of conflicts and regrets should melt away, leaving behind the memory of the underlying bond between you. In the early weeks of my grieving, my therapist predicted that this would happen, and I have found that to be true.

Early in my grieving process, I was lucky to meet a widower who also knew my husband well, and who gave me much good advice and comfort. One thing this widower told me was to "look for the love in this situation." I think that what he meant was to focus on the love we shared, and to use that as a source of strength. I found that to be important advice.

He suggested finding an artistic outlet, and spending at least two hours a day working creatively, without a major goal. He suggested spending at least 15 minutes a day, every day, writing about the intense feelings. I focused on writing a memoir and on playing the harp. Others might paint, or draw, or garden, or dance, or do craftwork. Whatever form the art takes, it should serve as a medium for expressing the emotions that come from within.

This widower and I checked in with each other every few days. That helped anchor me. I found it so valuable not only to get therapy, and to join a support group, but also to find at least one friend, and perhaps more than one, with whom to connect frequently on a one-to-one basis. This friend should be a person who understands the grieving process, from experience.

Physical exercise, yoga, massage, and meditation can also help. The whole self, body and soul, is involved in the grieving process. Therapy that is physical can help keep you grounded. Movement reminds the body that it needs to heal, too. Walk in a forest, and open your senses to the natural world around you. Try breathing slowly and deeply. Move in a way that uses the muscles and cardiovascular system at least once a day.

Grief is not a linear process. Many of us find ourselves revisiting emotions that we thought we had worked through already. Sometimes we revisit these emotions years after the death. There might be a trigger, something we encounter that suddenly elicits the old emotions, maybe an article of clothing, a snatch of music, a familiar scent. We work through the emotions, and they subside again. This is a normal part of the healing process.

The first time I felt myself laugh felt strange. My tear ducts had swollen in a way that seemed permanent, and my face had accommodated to expressions of pain. That day, something distracted me, and I smiled and laughed. I felt odd to use different muscles, and to let go. I felt almost guilty. But the sensation travelled through my body like a massage. Slowly, I began to realize that I could feel peace and joy again. He will always be with me, but I can feel joy. He would want that.

There are commonalities, but each person finds his or her own way to process grief. There is no right or wrong way, only the way that is best for you.

John writes:

PERMIT YOURSELF TO GRIEVE! Do not clench or suppress emotions associated with the death of your spouse so tightly that you become dysfunctional or ill. Doing so can drive survivors to adopt an approach/avoid strategy. Such a tactic can jeopardize the survivor's relationships with family and friends. Friends and family may be unable to ascertain what is really going on with the survivor.

Some widowed survivors may intentionally deny and squelch their emotional hurt. Some bury their pain deeply within themselves. Others try move on, as if nothing ever happened, projecting the impression they are over it. Nothing could be further from the truth and reality. **Denial of the pain of grief is absurd, but can serve a purpose for a temporary time.** As time goes on, the widowed survivor may regain their composure, confidence, and commitment to move ahead.

In the short, post-retirement months we had before Nancy's death, wherever you saw one of us the other was nearby. We maintained our individual schedules, activities, and hobbies, but frequently hung out together. It was a fantastic time. All was well! I was looking forward to growing old with my beautiful wife, but our time was cut short.

When describing our last wedding anniversary, she said, "this is the 34th of our first fifty years together, with an option to renew for another 50 years." I was beyond flattered that this wonderful, beautiful woman was willing to spend another 66 years with me. I knew I was loved, blessed, and wanted.

Then she died. Class began; no exams, tests, quizzes, or papers. Hit the ground running. I reeducated myself quickly to fully grasp the scope of the matters she handled, which I took for granted. While things were worked out during the period of post death turmoil, the experience was an odious ordeal I would never care to repeat. I was on a virtual journey of self-rediscovery, re-learning, and initial readjustment. I had a short, self-imposed learning curve. My life, as with any widowed survivor, will never again be the same.

The path of widowhood can be laden with pitfalls, frustrations, land mines, and oversights. My personal path has been lonely, frustrating, illuminating, challenging, demoralizing, and self-fulfilling; a tour I never wanted to begin, undertake, or experience. But, as with many bereaved survivors, I was at the mercy of fate; I had no choice.

In one-way conversations with my beloved Nancy (Yes, I still converse with her!) I say, **"Things were fine just as they were. Why did you have to leave me?"** Then, tearfully, I realize how much I really miss and still love her.

Widowed survivors try to project the image that they are devoid of physical, mental, emotional, or spiritual pain and distress. Realistically, no one can outrun grief. (See Chapter 1.3: "Physical and Emotional Sensations".) Grief relentlessly pursues and snags each of its individual victims. Grief traps them, leaves its brand, and demands a reckoning. Trying to portray a brave image in the heat of anguish can be complex, unhealthy, and excruciating.

Survivors generally become better able to manage their grief with the passage of time. As widowed survivors heal or develop improved coping skills, scar tissue develops over the wounded or broken heart. But remember, any unpredicted, random, unscheduled, or unexpected trigger can induce an emotional grief response and destroy the scar tissue. The catalyst could be a song, a comment, a scent, a situation, a lookalike, significant dates, events, anniversaries, or a memory. Any extraneous stimulus can ferociously rip the wound open and cause the widowed survivor to relive their pain and anguish without warning. The widowed survivor's mood and state of mind will vary from rage to resignation.

Dash the expectations, which expect a survivor to be back at work within in three days; smile as if everything is ok; put on a happy face; or, proclaim everything is fine.

"The heck I am. I'm in pain, the worst kind of pain I've ever experienced. There is no antidote! I do not wish this pain on anyone. I've passed through one of the most traumatic, worst experiences of my life. I am abandoned, dejected, hopeless, useless, spent, exhausted, empty, sad, fatigued, vindictive, out of touch in the surreal twilight zone, depleted, confused, alone, afraid, unlovable, out of options, and extremely angry."

It's easier to go into shut down and denial. Grieving a spouse's death and widowhood both hurt. Grief and mourning test each survivor's limits. **"I don't care about anything. I**

want the world to go away. Let me wad up into a little ball and retreat to the depths and darkness of my sanctuary. I feel safe and secure here. This place is my sacred retreat and fortification. I can cry here if I desire. If I'm angry about something, like the stupid remarks people make, I can reckon with it or yell at them in my own privacy, while reflecting they are mostly trying to be helpful."

Many widowed survivors have suggested and perceived that the comments by the uninformed supporters, meant to be helpful, are thoughtless, careless, inappropriate, and aggravating. (Further discussion follows in Chapter 4.7: "Coping with Those Who Say or Do the Wrong Thing".) Eventually widowed survivors may reach a point in their grief where they find the grace to forgive dimwitted comments uttered by family and friends. But also remember some friends and family will also disappear and never return.

For some newly widowed survivors, anger, rage, and yelling are normal reactions. Sometimes, in their solitude, survivors need to release their pent up feelings. The Old Testament books of Job, Psalms, Lamentations, Numbers, Exodus, Joel, Ezekiel, Micah, Habakkuk, and Ecclesiastes are useful references. The New Testament versions of the Gospels are also helpful.

Widowed survivors should consider "be good to and take care of yourself". The New Testament quotes Jesus saying, "Love one another as I have loved you and love your neighbor as yourself."

Coping – getting on with life – some never do. Death of a loved one can mark the end of the sense of personal centeredness and the widowed survivor's universe. Why? (See Chapter 3.4: "Grieving Styles".)

- Some survivors never recover from losing the love of their life.

- Some survivors feel uneasy and unsecure about going out as a "single" person.
- Some survivors feel guilty at the prospect of potentially betraying their deceased spouse if they become romantically involved with another person.
- Some survivors believe they might be unlovable.
- Some survivors welcome opportunities to socialize with others but want to remain unencumbered to enjoy their newly found independence.
- Some survivors are lost, overwhelmed, and lack the initiative, confidence, or ability to "get their act together."
- Some expect to replicate the level and type of love they had with their deceased spouse. But, that past love cannot be matched.

But remember, **LOVE NEVER DIES!**

3.4 Grieving Styles

Kathy writes:

A grieving style is a pattern of behaviors that a person tends to use in grieving, based on their personality. For example, some people express grief by thinking, problem-solving, and taking action. Others express grief by releasing emotions. Some express anger; others tend to express sorrow. Some wish to be alone. Others seek out support from others. The behaviors can vary from time to time, but a grieving style is the general tendency of a particular individual.

A grieving style can be influenced by culture, individual history, and genetics. The result is a style that is individual, and is subject to change over time. Categorizing people to predict how they will grieve is unrealistic, because it is such an individual process. Deciding how people *should* grieve is also unrealistic. There is no incorrect grieving style.

In his book *Helping Grieving People – When Tears Are Not Enough,* Jeffreys (2011) lists and describes seven principles of human grief.   One of the most important principles is that there is no one right way to grieve.

The release of emotions can be a cathartic and healing process. Grief therapy is available for survivors to explore their feelings and release their emotions. Grief support groups should provide a supportive atmosphere for widows and widowers to share their feelings and experiences. These support systems are most helpful to those who more easily release their emotions, or who seek out support from others.

But some people are less comfortable in expressing grief by revealing their emotions or sharing their experiences with support groups. Friends and relatives of those who are grieving need to respect each person's grieving style, and not pass judgment. Likewise, those who are grieving should not pass judgment on themselves. Those who do not easily grieve by outwardly expressing emotion can seek out an environment that feels safe to them for times when they do wish to express emotion. If the emotions are overwhelming, they can find ways to express it in smaller doses. They might need a more private expression of grief, rather than support groups. They might express their grief more easily with action, rather than words. Rituals can benefit those who express emotion by taking action. Physical exercise can provide a release of energy. The use of books and videos might be more useful to those who express their grief by thinking things through.

Another important principle of human grief described in Jeffreys' book is that there is no universal timetable for grief. Others might get impatient with how long it takes us to grieve, but their impatience is irrelevant. The time needed to grieve is determined by the one grieving. The process takes as long as the one grieving needs it to take.

One of the common myths associated with grief is the idea that the grief proceeds through fixed stages – namely, denial, anger, bargaining, depression, and acceptance. These stages were borrowed from Elisabeth Kübler-Ross's 1969 book *On Death and Dying*. In that book, Kübler-Ross describes experiences that patients go through when facing death. They were not stages of grief, but stages of facing death. Others have extended this model to describe many other situations, including the grief process of survivors. Even Kübler-Ross admitted that those who are dying do not necessarily experience these stages in order, nor do they necessarily experience all the stages. Often people switch between stages or return to previous stages. A number of researchers and organizations have argued against the idea that grief must occur in stages.

Both the style of grief and the stages and timing of the grieving process are individual. The person who is grieving knows best how to grieve, and how long it will take. No one else has the right to tell you how you should grieve, whether you should go through certain stages, or how long it should take.

John writes:

Widowed survivors grieve publically and privately. Open expression of personal grief helps release deeply buried regrets, guilt, and pain.

A grief journey (See Chapter 1.2: "Sudden Loss vs. Lingering Illness".) is an arduous adventure.   The excursion involves crawling through a dark tunnel laden with primeval muck and ooze into an unknown future. Grief cannot be donated, dismissed, or detonated. Grief's devastation can be remedied by deciding to move ahead with life. Others relieve their grief by retreating into a sheltered, private cocoon to shut the world out.   No survivor escapes or outruns the grief journey, no matter how hard they may try. Many attempt to flee, preferring to forget. They would openly welcome support, comfort, and relief. Widowed survivors instinctively seem to know for certain they will embark on the inevitable grief journey.

Survivors may ask:
- Will someone ever love me unconditionally for who I am despite my flaws, unsavory habits, and moodiness?
- Will I ever dare to risk loving again?
- Is there someone who just wants to be with me and who wants me to be with them?
- Can I ever meet someone whom I will trust enough to be honest and open with me again, in a state of mutual acceptance and respect?
- Will I ever be able to meet someone with whom I can enjoy love, affection and just be myself?

- Is there anyone with whom I can mutually share my deepest thoughts, desires, fears, trepidations, and feel safe in doing so without fear of ridicule, judgment, attribution, retribution, or rejection?
- Do I want to remarry, or do I only want the benefit of having a few close friends and the opportunity to see them regularly?
- Do I want to live out my days in solitude, isolation, or self-imposed loneliness?

Survivors may pose these questions in their search for connections. They should also not become so inhibited that they forget to move ahead with their lives. Exercising discretion and caution are very important considerations. But reaching out to others and letting new friendships evolve, grow, and develop also offer some significant benefits. Don't become overly dependent on finding the right answers to all of these questions with any degree of immediacy.

I recommend that each survivor follow individual instincts, keep an open mind, and embrace the opportunity to enjoy pursuing a new life. The transition may be at a slower pace than you might like. But spontaneity can generate a multitude of wonderful opportunities for socializing, rebuilding personal confidence, and finding enjoyment. Being lonely is generally a choice. Usually one only has to reach out.

3.5 Thoughts of Suicide or Self-Harm

Kathy writes:

Thoughts of suicide are common among widows and widowers, especially during the early stages of grief. There is a big difference between thinking about suicide and actually acting on those thoughts. Call 1-800-273-TALK (8255), the National Suicide Prevention Lifeline, available 25 hours, 7 days a week, if you need to talk to someone about your thoughts or urges. Counselors are prepared to listen to any of a variety of issues, even just loneliness.

I sat next to a widower at a grief support group one night, when he chose to tell me about his suicide attempt. He had actually gone through with an attempt to take his own life, but had been discovered and saved. He said that he would not try it again.

And I remember my own thoughts of suicide. But I did not make a specific plan about how I would go about it. To me that was a sign that I was likely not to act on my thoughts. I thought about the two cats that my husband had left behind, that he had loved dearly, and who depended on me completely for their care. Ultimately, this is what kept me going. I could not imagine what they would do without me. The grief process is so intense in the beginning that sometimes it is difficult to understand how one can survive it. But it might help us to think about the creatures, and the people, who would be hurt, even devastated, if we committed suicide.

Knowing that the intensity of grief subsides over time can help us to bear it now. Widows and widowers who are further along in the process sometimes tell us that we don't "get over" the loss. And that is true. But the intensity does subside. And joy will happen again. Life becomes interesting again.

If you are the concerned friend or relative of a new widow or widower, please pay special attention to the grieving person in the early months and weeks. Call them, invite them to dinner, take them places, tell them you love them, and tell them how important they are in your life.

If you are the widow or widower, read all you can about grief, so that you will understand it. Contact your local hospice or hospital to find grief support groups. Find a grief counselor. Find grief blogs and chat rooms on the web. Turn to the "Resources" chapter in the back of this book.

John writes:

I sought counseling after Nancy died. I was dealing with many issues related to abandonment, anger, depression, guilt, despondence, self-pity, PTSD, hypervigilance, regret, remorse, self-doubt, loss of personal self-confidence, and low self-esteem. (See Chapter 3.3: "The Emotional Stuff".)

During a counseling session, my counselor asked if I had thought of harming myself after Nancy's death. I responded in the affirmative, but quickly explained the thought was only a fleeting notion. I clarified that self-harm conflicted with my personal moral code, religious beliefs, and spirituality. The thought flashed across my mind, shortly after her death, because now I was suddenly alone in the world for the first time. My life had changed forever. It seemed for a moment life would have been easier to still be with Nancy. But, she was never coming back. Something inside me told me I needed to move on with my life.

I have learned since the counseling session that many newly widowed survivors admitted to contemplating self-harm immediately after the death of their spouse. Why? Because the overpowering shock and anguish caused by the death of their spouse totally stunned and clouded their judgment. Fleeting suicidal or physical self-harm ideations may be more prevalent among newly widowed survivors than previously thought. Fortunately, most new survivors make no gesture or attempt at self-harm. Many have pains from their loss that ache so deeply, some will pursue almost any means, shy of attempted suicide, to achieve relief and salve their wounds. Some self soothe by resorting to excessive alcohol use, substance or medication abuse, self-mutilation, or personal self-neglect.

Dr. Joan Shirley, a former colleague, well-reputed special educator and psychologist, shared some interesting observations. She conjectures that sometimes the road ahead seems bleak and devoid of purpose or joy. She affirms there is no quick abdication of this sorrow and that the inability to unburden one-self creates an uncertain, insecure, and unguaranteed future. She observes, for consolation, individuals may turn to self-destructive behavior, to a prayerful conversation with God, or seek support from their families. All of these powerful potions may collide at one time.

Dr. Shirley surmises, "I believe my God assures me of His ongoing faithfulness and love. This love is not dependent on the resident contentment I may have previously known. The love is part of a further journey orchestrated by Him to use me and my talents for His purposes. At times I feel alone and abandoned, but my faith tells me I can count on and trust in His continued presence, limitless mercy and unconditional love."

3.6 Communication, Signs, and Synchronicity

Kathy writes:

Communication with those near to us who have died is a very common experience. This can take place directly, in visions or dreams, when the loved one gives us a message, or embraces us, or simply appears. Or it can happen indirectly, with signs or synchronicity.

A sign is an event that signifies a deeper meaning than the event itself. Sometimes people ask for a sign that all is well with their loved one, and then shortly after that, they observe an unusual event. For example, I read about someone who saw butterflies after she had attended the funeral of someone she loved. She interpreted the appearance of the butterflies as a sign, a communication from her loved one to indicate that all was well.

Synchronicity is a term that was invented by Carl Jung, to indicate the occurrence of two or more events at the same time, or nearly the same time, in a way that indicates meaning to the one experiencing the events. Without the meaning, the two events might be called coincidence, but with the meaning, they become synchronicity. For example, someone might experience a power outage in their house, and later discover that the outage happened at the exact moment of death of a loved one in a distant city. The survivor might interpret the outage as a message, and take comfort from it.

I don't think it's that important to try to figure out whether what you've experienced is a direct communication, or a sign, or synchronicity. What is important is that these events are very common, natural, and normal, and you do not have to be a professional psychic to experience them. What is important is that there is meaning and comfort to draw from these experiences.

At the same time, if you do not experience these events, I hope you will not feel cheated or frustrated. Sometimes the communications are very subtle, and it takes sensitivity, openness, and patience to recognize them. Sometimes someone else might have dreams about your loved one, and will tell you about the dreams. That's still a communication, even though it came indirectly through someone else's dream. You can find more satisfaction if you do not have expectations, but simply remain open.

I have chosen never to demand communication. I do not want to pull back anyone from things that they need to do in the afterlife. I want to let them do what they need to do. Instead, I allow myself to be open to them if they wish to communicate with me. A couple of times I did ask for signs, but those are exceptions.

I will describe a few of my experiences below.

Only three weeks after Dennis's death, I had a dream in which Dennis appeared. The dream took place in my brother's island house. I was searching for some answers and trying to figure out how to contact an old friend. Dennis came into the room and saw my concern. He took me by the feet and held me upside down so that the answers would flow out of me. Then I lay on the floor, and noticed that it was just Dennis and me, and somehow that seemed to be the answer. This all took place in the large room surrounded by windows facing the bay.

About a month after his death, while I was still in bed, I had an experience that did not seem like a dream. I felt as if I were awake. I heard human footsteps come lightly up the stairs, pause, and then go back downstairs. Then I heard light sounds from downstairs, and I sensed a presence there. The experience seemed real, and perfectly natural, and I wasn't afraid at all, but felt protected. The event felt like times when I used to hear Dennis walking around early on a Saturday morning while I was still sleeping or in a near-sleep state. But as I said, the experience seemed very real, and I felt that I was awake. I told this story to a grief support group the next day, and two women seemed to know exactly what I was talking about. One woman said simply, with certainty, "It was real." The other woman told of experiences she had when she felt as if her late husband was in bed with her. She said at those times she tried not to move, so that the experience would stay with her for a while.

I had a dream early Christmas morning, a little over a year after Dennis's death, which seemed extraordinary and left me with a good feeling. The dream seemed to take place in the front hall of my parents' house. Dennis was there with me in the hall, and we were singing a gospel bluegrass song together. The song was about sleep and dreaming, and how beautiful and wonderful it was to sleep and dream. I remarked to myself how beautiful his voice sounded, and how wonderful it was to share music with him. The tune to the song was still ringing in my head when I awoke, and I could still almost hear it as I wrote down the dream. I felt the dream to be my Christmas present from Dennis.

Later I thought that the melody was similar to a bluegrass gospel tune. I found the entire song on the web -- *A Beautiful Life*, by William M. Golden, written in 1918. When I read the lyrics to that song, I realized that they referred in a subtle way to life after death. This song fit in so well with the spirit of the dream. The dream left me with a peaceful feeling. It felt like a gift.

On his birthday, five and a half years after his death, just before I awoke, Dennis came to me in a dream. I was singing a long and beautiful song. Dennis was sitting next to me, and he was so moved by the song, and he was singing along too, with emotion on his face, but he sang so quietly that I could hardly hear his voice.

What did it mean? He was still with me, but I barely heard his voice. Maybe I would ask to hear his voice more clearly.

Three months later, I had a dream about Dennis that was not as pleasant as many others. In the dream, he was dancing with a woman, doing a side step down a narrow aisle between two rows of benches, away from me, towards the back of the large room. I felt some feelings of sadness. When I awoke, it occurred to me that this place was like a church, and I had been sitting in front of the pews, and Dennis was dancing down the aisle, in the opposite direction from a wedding procession. Maybe it symbolized his death, his leaving me.

That same day, something strange happened. I was driving to an appointment, when I decided to turn on the radio. I had not turned on the radio in months, maybe even years, because the settings for accessing favorite stations had been erased. But I turned it on anyway, used the seek button a few times, and suddenly I heard a piece of classical orchestral music that sounded so familiar. As I listened, I slowly realized that Dennis and I had listened to this piece several times, over and over. Each phrase was so familiar, and so lush and beautiful. I sat in the parking garage to hear the ending and the announcement of what the piece was. I felt sure it was a composition by Robert Schumann. Finally the announcer said it was Robert Schumann's *Symphony # 4*. That symphony was one of our most favorite pieces of orchestral music. Later as I told my grief therapist about this, I said that it was as if Dennis had guided me to that music, and was speaking to me. She said that it definitely seemed to be a communication, and said that perhaps Dennis was comforting me after that dream that I experienced.

I think that I experienced communications and signs much more frequently in the early weeks and months after Dennis's death. During that time, my feelings were much more intense, and I more desperately needed the comfort from those communications. It's possible that he has moved on to a higher plane of existence than in the beginning. But I still have dreams about him even now. I feel that he is always with me.

John writes:

This section may separate readers into three categories: Believers, Skeptics, or Cynics. Discussion within this chapter is not an attempt to stress a particular point of view. I am writing about my personal perceptions, recollections, beliefs, and experiences.

Some survivors (**believers**) claim to have received communications and signs from their departed spouses. Others (**cynics**) suggest such phenomena are imagined or impossible. Some (**skeptics**) disbelieve any such thing is impossible without pragmatic, tangible evidence or proof.

Believers, who have experienced unusual phenomena, claim their experiences were real and seemed plausible. The believers have not attempted nor suggested what others should feel or believe.

I have had dreams, heard sounds, whiffed scents, and received signs, which some might claim could be dismissed as coincidence. But I consider my experiences real. They were not precipitated nor induced by use of hallucinogens, alcohol consumption, or mind-altering substances.

On more than one occasion, I have heard Nancy's voice calling my name or reminding me to wake up. I have felt and perceived signs of her presence around me. I have communicated with her in dreams. In the dreams, she has both expressed her wishes for me to get on with my life and given her blessing for me to do so.

When she died, I was searching for the clothes for her burial. I searched closets and found none of her garments. Perhaps I was blinded in my grief-stricken emotion and did not see what was really there. Or maybe things really weren't there.

The morning after Nancy's death, I met with the funeral director at the mortuary to finalize arrangements. Before leaving home, I opened the same hallway entry closet door, which I searched the previous evening. To my astonishment, as if they had purposely been placed there, I found the clothes for which I had previously searched. I found an array of her favorite blouses, sweaters, and other garments. I admit the clothes may have been hanging there the night before and I may have overlooked them. However, I choose to believe Nancy's spirit intervened.

Things I have heard, dreamt, seen, and noted are factual and true to the best of my recollection, perception, and experience. Events that transpired after Nancy's death remain very real to me. I hold crystal clear memories of them. During the week after she died, I was awakened every morning by Nancy's voice calling to me and saying "John, get up". Other times I heard the doorbell ring several times, went to answer the door, and found no one was there. I know what I heard.

I had a remarkable dream, which seemed like a visitation. In the dream my beautiful Nancy was smiling, her beautiful deep blue eyes were sparkling. She crawled into bed, wearing one of my favorite dress shirts – she liked to sleep in my shirts. She announced, "I'm pregnant". To my credibility, I knew this was impossible.

The dream occurred a month before I moved. I prayed and meditated about the dream. I interpreted the dream's message as Nancy's blessing and permission to get on with the rest of my life. I concluded she was happy, content, in a good place, and around me.

In December 2015, I was lamenting the prospect of spending another Christmas alone. A thought or notion popped into my mind pronouncing: "This is the third Christmas you are shutting out the holiday. I gave you my blessing to get on with your life in 2013 after I died, and you have not. I'll always be your Cinderella, the girl to whom you gave the crystal slipper. But when the Lord called, I clicked my ruby slippers to go home. I'll always be here, but you have to let me go. I can't move on until you release me. I have things to do. I'll always love you, but you've got to finish your work and let me go to do mine."

I have worn my wife's wedding band on my right hand since 2013. She'd "lost" it about seven months prior to her death. The fact that she couldn't find it bothered her. I only found the ring, after she died, when I was preparing to put the house on the market before my move.

Recently I was out for an evening with friends. When I returned home that evening, I realized the ring was missing from my finger. To my chagrin, I did not find the ring after searching the house, the driveway, the porch and the car twice. I traced and retraced my steps multiple times – no ring! I finally concluded the ring was gone and could have been lost anywhere. But I know it was on my finger when I left home that evening.

Two nights later, when I pulled out the chair to sit down to do some work at the computer, the ring was sitting on the chair cushion. I know the ring was not there before, as I had worked at the computer during those two days. I don't know how the ring came to be on the chair cushion, but there it was and I put it back on my finger.

I have experienced other dreams and received other signs that convince me our deceased beloved are with us.

I have spoken with some survivors (skeptics) who deny such things are possible without tangible proof. To their credit, they want discrete, hard physical evidence. Some survivors (cynics) believe no type of communication or sign from "the beyond" is possible; "once you're dead, you're dead".

Individuals should remain true to their beliefs and values with regard to the paranormal, life after death, and communications from beyond. No point of view is more correct than the other.

3.7 Strength from Spiritual Practice

Kathy writes:

Spiritual practice is a very personal choice. Some people derive their spiritual practices from organized religion. Others find their spiritual practice outside of organized religion. Still others do both. Regardless of the form that it takes, a spiritual practice can be very powerful in helping one to work through grief.

As we explained in the introduction to this book, in some ways John and I have very different philosophies and spiritual practices. We respect each other's differences, and each of us chooses not to proselytize. When we describe our stories in this book, it is not with the intent to prescribe what others should do or believe, but only to describe our story, with the hope that the reader will take from it what might work for that reader.

The community of those who have lost a partner is a very diverse community. When we come together to support each other, the emphasis is on support. Support for each other requires that we learn tolerance for the differences in the viewpoints of each of us, listen to each other, and perhaps even enjoy our differences and learn from them.

What John and I have both found in common is that having a spiritual practice can help in the grieving process. A spiritual practice can help center the grieving person at a time when everything else seems to be falling apart. A spiritual practice can serve as a very calming, healing, comforting anchor. The type of spiritual practice must be one that works for the particular individual who practices it.

Much of my own spiritual practice is based on connection with nature. I spent much time in the woods as a child, and found much solace there. I still have my copy of the children's book based on St. Francis of Assisi's *Canticle of the Sun*, with its stunning illustrations by Elizabeth Orton Jones. When I walk through a forest, or along a beach, I stop thinking or talking about concerns outside what is here, in this forest or on this beach, right now. Instead, I open my senses to full awareness, in the present moment, and find connection with the divine that runs through all nature. The walk through the forest or along the beach becomes a meditation or a prayer.

In the early 1970s, I learned a meditation practice from India that helped to center me and give me strength. I still sometimes use that practice. I can use it at any time, but find it most valuable when I am feeling as if my world is falling apart. I can attain a sense of connection with the divine, and feelings of balance and stability.

Later, in the 1990s, Dennis and I learned a Chinese self-healing practice called qigong. Through qigong, one reaches out to gather healing energy from nature and then directs the energy towards oneself, in order to heal. We were able to connect this with our experiences in nature by sensing the healing energy of nature, pulling in this energy, and using it for healing. One time we stood on the beach at the Pacific Ocean, practicing qigong in concert with the movement of the ocean waves. That was a very powerful experience. I find that I can use these practices now, for spiritual as well as physical healing.

Even in my childhood, I heard even the most conventional theologians say that God does not have gender. They told us that the divine is infinite and transcends the human distinction between male and female. And yet from that time until now, male images of God have predominated in our culture and our language. To balance this, I seek out images of the feminine face of God. Or I seek out the genderless divine that can be found in experiences within nature or meditation. I find much healing in these experiences.

Dennis's death was a shattering experience. But in the face of this shattering, my spiritual practice helped to center me and provide strength from within.

John writes:

Widowed survivors pursue their spiritual practice differently. Some find strength in prayer during difficult times. Others find peace through meditation, discernment, or introspection. The death of a spouse harshly challenges the spiritual belief systems of the widowed survivor.

Some widowed survivors have little or no regard for spiritual practice. They disavow belief in any higher order deity, and reject the notion of an afterlife. They believe death is the natural end to mortal life and hold no belief in any sort of afterlife. They find validation by giving life a good run and by living every day to its fullest.

Some survivors pursue spirituality privately, independently, and individually. They connect with their God or higher source when and as they feel the need. They may or may not have engaged in organized religion.

Some survivors are affiliated with established religious congregations and groups who worship through formal services. They read from the Bible, Talmud, Torah, or other sacred texts and teachings. They observe traditional religious practice and ritual publically and privately.

Many turn to religious beliefs and spirituality for inspiration and comfort in their search for relief, answers, and resolution. Some may feel abandoned or enraged at their deity (God). Many seek inner peace, understanding, and healing. Spiritual practice can help remedy pain, restore a sense of balance, improve coping skills, and reinforce the desire to continue.

Sometimes insensitive individuals violate another's value system by openly criticizing personal, religious, or spiritual beliefs. When overly sensitive survivors perceive the critical comments as personal criticisms or attacks, they may temporarily withdraw to avoid conflict. Sometimes disagreements occur within families where the spouses had different religious beliefs, cultural values, or ethnic backgrounds.

Bereaved survivors can be mutually supportive by trying to understand others' values, customs, and belief systems. Along the path of the grief journey, survivors are in pursuit of peace, recovery, and healing. Resiliency will eventually come to the widowed searcher.

For personal healing and understanding, I read the Old Testament and New Testament biblical scriptures. My favorite Old Testament references include the books of Wisdom, Job, Exodus, Lamentations, Habakkuk, Nahum, Ecclesiastes, Psalms, and Proverbs. These Old Testament writings tell the stories of people who experienced calamity in their lives, but who persevered in their faith under some very adverse conditions. But they persevered.

The New Testament highlights the continuing human search for spiritual meaning, guidance, love, and peace. Readings cite the teachings of Jesus, examples of his ministry and the times he sought respite for personal prayer, reflection, and rest. Even in biblical times, people endured and questioned pain, suffering, hardship, and calamity. Life was not always fair.

These readings discuss personal grief, joy, prayer, regret, reflection, bereavement, and renewal. Will I ever heal? Why God? Why me? Does God really love me? Why would a God of limitless mercy and love permit such harsh tribulation, suffering, and affliction to vex me? What have I done to anger Him? I didn't ask to be here. Will it ever stop? Total trust, surrender…the travesty is beyond me. I can't fix it. I don't want to accept it. I don't understand it. How will I survive this? Personal reflection on the Book of Exodus, the story of Israelites' journey through the desert for 40 years, reaffirms my belief and hope that I will eventually exit the wilderness.

Persons of every culture, creed, and religious belief faith pursue "God". People derive strength through spiritual practices, readings, beliefs, and customs. Respecting each widowed survivor's beliefs is paramount.

In personal prayer, I seek forgiveness, love, mercy, wisdom, guidance, discernment, peace, hope, faith, and acceptance to regain personal composure and my sense of wholeness.

My personal prayer for healing is: *Father God, please give me what I need as I walk with Jesus along the path to wherever the Holy Spirit is leading. Your will be done not mine. Amen.*

Part 4. Learning to Cope

Part 4 describes the shift that occurs after the initial adjustment, as the survivor learns to cope with the loss of the partner. It is very common for survivors to experience issues with feelings of guilt, with change, with relationships with children, or with childlessness. There are also uncommon issues that might cause the survivor to feel alone, as if no one else could be experiencing the same problems. But there are many strategies that can decrease the sense of aloneness. Part 4 describes these strategies, identifies methods that helped us to cope, and refers to other resources.

4.1 Now What Do I Do

Kathy writes:

Part 3 of this book describes the initial adjustment to the death of a spouse, when emotions are at their most intense, and there are pressing practical issues. Part 4 provides suggestions about learning to cope, after the initial adjustment. Now all the relatives and friends from out of town have left, ceremonies have been held, people and businesses have been notified, and you have managed to survive. But now you are left with yourself. What do you actually do about it?

What you do now depends on your individual grieving style and your needs. Now is the time to be selfish. That might seem wrong, but you have been shattered, you need healing, and you can help others only by loving yourself first. If you find it overwhelming to go to a wedding or to a funeral, don't go. A close friend of my husband died in the year after his death. I could not bring myself to go to the funeral. I was still in a raw state, and I knew I would be sobbing instead of offering support to the grieving spouse. Taking care of yourself is the right thing to do. On the other hand, if you really want to go on a vacation adventure but feel guilty about having a good time, go. You deserve to have a good time and to heal.

If you are totally alone and isolated, ask your closest friend or relative to call you every day. Join a grief support group, or join several such groups. Join groups that share your specific interests. Refer to the "Resources" section at the end of this book for a description of support groups and Meetup groups and how to access them. Find somewhere to go several times a week. Find new friends who are understanding and supportive. If old acquaintances, friends, or relatives are not understanding and supportive, make changes. You will need to decide whether to explain your needs to others who lack understanding, or find time apart.

If you are overwhelmed with people, and need to be alone, then seek out alone time. Or perhaps you need only change the people with whom you associate. You might discover that your time with others feels better when the others are those who truly understand and are supportive. On the other hand, perhaps you do need more solitude. Listen to your inner self and follow its guidance.

Consider not making any major changes for at least a year or two. As I mentioned in an earlier chapter, when my husband died, I immediately thought about quitting my job. But then I realized that it would be too big a change, just after the big change of his death. So I compromised, and decided to go part-time. This worked out well. I worked part-time for another year and a half, and then retired. I discovered supportive people at work who surprised me. Some of them had experienced their own losses. We were able to share our stories, and I felt less alone. The work was interesting and it was a good decision financially.

Find ways to memorialize your spouse. When Dennis died, I wanted so much to always remember him, and for him to be remembered by others. So I started writing a memoir about our life together. I know that I will be able to read it to remember, even if I have memory loss in later years. And maybe one day I will publish a version of it. Some websites for grief support dedicate space for survivors to post writing and photographs of their loved ones for others to see. There was no gravesite for Dennis's remains, so I installed a memorial stone in the nature center where we both often hiked together. Some survivors plant memorial trees in parks. Some establish memorial scholarship funds. These are actions you can take that can be so gratifying.

When your emotions are strong, find ways to release them. Create an altar in a special place in your house, with photographs, special mementos, and perhaps a candle. Once a day, sit in front of your altar and release your emotions. Cry, talk to your loved one, or meditate. You might discover that this release results in more peace and calm during the rest of your day, as I did.

Visit a grief counselor to talk through your emotions and concerns. If the counselor does not seem to understand and support you, find another one who does. Ask other widows and widowers for suggestions about whom to work with.

I think I found most solace by joining several widow/widowers' groups. These people have also experienced the loss of their spouse, so they "get it". They understand what it is like, they are supportive, they might have good suggestions, and some of them become real friends.

John writes:

Learning to cope with the death of a spouse can be a hard, cruel ordeal or an adventurous challenge. Each survivor must decide individually which course they wish to pursue. At times making the choice poses a dilemma. In the 1970s we said, "Today is the first day of the rest of your life." Losing my spouse spurred me to ask, "Do I wallow, walk in a fog, live in a hopeless vacuum, or choose to survive?"

The impact of experiencing the death of a spouse has been discussed previously. The tragedy has given each widowed survivor sufficient background to write and publish their own story because each is an expert in grief, loss, and coping.

Some of the questions and comments listed below may assist survivors to find their bearings.
- Am I losing my mind or am I down in the dumps?
- Where am I emotionally?
- It seems some days I cannot go on. What drives me to continue?
- What do I believe about the old saying, "God doesn't give you more than you can handle"? I get up in the morning and usually crawl out of bed; sometimes not. Some days I don't want to go on but I do and I will.
- What has worked for others? What has worked for me, but not for others? What has not worked for me that worked for others?
- What does my grief journey look like now?
- How do I express my grief?
- Do I dare express and/or share my grief with others or do I bottle it up?
- How do I react to those who try to tell me how to grieve?
- How am I coping?
- Have I sought, engaged, or received treatment, counseling, or therapy for my grief? What are my concerns and issues?
- What has been most helpful? How has the information been beneficial and useful?

- What has been most helpful on my grief journey? What has been least helpful?
- What have been (are) my stages of grief?
- What does my grief journey look like?
- What do I believe distinguishes grief, bereavement, and mourning?
- Do I have or do I want to make room in my life for anyone else besides myself?
- Am I sad or depressed? Am I both sad and depressed? Do I understand the differences between sadness and depression?

Deciding to continue living is a choice, not a mandate. The decision rests with the individual survivor's attitude, motivation, and demeanor.

Survivors with children who still live at home will generally be spurred on because of their obligations and responsibilities. They will muster the energy needed to honor and fulfill their duties. Most childless survivors, or those who have older children, will generally choose to move ahead. A few survivors, overwhelmed by their grief, will sink into the morass and retreat from the challenges and opportunities afforded by their new reality, choosing to remain static.

4.2 Regrets and Guilt and Dealing with Them

Kathy writes:

When my husband died, I was tormented by feelings of guilt, and I thought I was the only one. I soon discovered that these feelings are so common among widows and widowers that they are nearly universal. That discovery in itself provided some healing for me. But I needed more.

My husband died suddenly and completely unexpectedly, in the middle of the night. I was sleeping right next to him, but suddenly awoke and realized something was wrong. I tried to awaken him, but could not. I called 911. I tried to resuscitate him, but could not. I had never taken CPR or first aid. For months, I carried around with me terrible guilt that I could not resuscitate him.

I went to an urgent care physician when I got shingles. Somehow the death of my husband came up. I described his state of health and confessed my feelings of guilt to the physician. She told me that she understood his health condition, that she used to be an emergency room physician, and that I could not have resuscitated him unless I had a defibrillator in the room! That was very reassuring.

I have also experienced guilty feelings about things I said, things I wish I had done, and things I would have done differently if I knew he had so little time left. Slowly, slowly, with the help of other widows and widowers who tell me their own stories of guilt feelings, I am releasing the feelings.

Worrying about what you should have done in the past is never productive. The past cannot be changed. Planning what you will change in the future is much more productive. I

always say that the phrase "should have" should not be in the
English language.

I know that in my mind, but it isn't always easy to connect my
feelings with what I know intellectually. So I remind myself.
And I use a releasing technique that Dennis himself showed
me. Refer to the "Resources" section of this book for a book
written by Dwoskin, called *The Sedona Method.* It consists of
a simple series of questions you ask yourself, to guide
yourself into the experience of letting go.

Sometimes it helps to have a conversation with the one who
has died. Many times after his death, I found myself telling
Dennis that I loved him and forgave him, and asking him to
forgive me. I found this to be a healing experience.

Other ways to release guilty feelings include talking with other
widows/widowers with similar feelings, talking with a therapist,
or talking with a trusted spiritual counselor.

John writes:

Widowed survivors harbor regrets and guilt associated with
the death of their spouse. Such realization or overly obsessive
self-reflection may drive some to become cynical, ambivalent,
lethargic, and self-unforgiving about many past events,
situations, and circumstances in which they wish they acted
differently. Their remorse may haunt every waking moment.
Some survivors scrupulously hold themselves to high
standards of reparation for their perceived wrongs. These
regrets comprise the platform from which their guilt trip
departs.

We become hypercritical of our past conduct, attitudes, and
reactions to things our deceased spouse did to provoke us. To
gain a sense of personal peace, we want to overcompensate
by forgiving and overlooking almost everything that infuriated

us. This behavior reflects a tendency directed at salving our wounds, soothing our regrets, and alleviating our guilty feelings. But how can efforts directed at atonement help now? We know nothing we do will bring our deceased spouse back to us.

We are ashamed of snide remarks and scathing criticisms voiced because of our displeasure over some inconsequential matter, which seemed seriously major at the time. In the aftermath of death, the regrettable matter is trivial, pointlessly minute, and poignantly forgettable. We labor over the pains of the minutiae trying to remedy the unfixable.

After self-reflection, we may rationalize that we never intended to be hurtful. Since our spouse is dead, we can no longer say "I love you" or "I'm sorry." We internalize sorrows and regrets; feeling the need to punish ourselves. The only absolutions to be gained are in self-forgiveness and in the belief that our spouse forgives us.

The natural dynamic of living together causes people to interact sometimes lovingly, and at other times coldly. Guilt drives survivors to assume the roles of prosecutor, judge, jury, and executioner. The sense of closure we seek is nowhere to be found. It is difficult to take back any remark once it has been spoken. Comments and reactions meant to reflect displeasure, unhappiness, and criticism struck their target. In retrospect, we are upset with ourselves and want to recant everything.

Some of the following comments may reflect the spirit of reticent guilt. Survivors with whom I have spoken generally agree with the accuracy and relevance of these reflections.

"Think before you speak because loose lips sink ships".
One's tongue can slash another so deeply that it cuts like a knife, inflicting severe anguish and pain. Alternatives are to

remain silent or to avoid commenting in the passion of the
moment.

"Think of the consequences of any action you may take".
Your deed may be interpreted as crushing disapproval,
devastating criticism, or abject rejection by the recipient,
especially your spouse. Be assured if you intend to be cruel
or mean, the intended victim knows. We painstakingly make
sure they do! Think before you act. Remove yourself from the
heat of the moment. Take a self-imposed time-out.

**"If you don't intend for something you have written to see
the light of day, do not write it."** This is especially apropos
since we communicate in a world of notes, emails, texts, the
internet, and social media. Once posted, interpretation rests
with the recipient and anyone else who may have access. The
meanings of words are in people, not in the dictionary.
Inflammatory communications, drafted under tense
circumstances, reflect our demeanor at that time. Avoid
overreacting to the controversial, heated intensity of a
situation. Think and take time before writing, commenting, or
responding. In fact, after drafting any written response, put it
aside, walk away, and come back later. Review the rant and if
you still feel the urge to do so, send it, amend it, or consider
deleting it.

The above thoughts are in retrospect. The survivor's spouse
is dead and the past cannot be undone. Many may would
have preferred to never have said, written, or done some of
these regrettable things. They realize the absurdity of their
conduct!

I reflect on certain events and situations within our marriage
and second-guess how I might have handled certain situations
differently. Things that will never be, apologies, dashed plans,
and failed dreams have become a lost Camelot.

4.3 Changes and Getting Overwhelmed

Kathy writes:

The death of a spouse is a huge change. The Holmes and Rahe Stress Scale ranks the death of a spouse as the most stressful of all life events. The Holmes and Rahe Stress Scale is a test that measures risk of illness based on what stressful experiences have taken place in the past year in the test-taker's life. The test includes a list of life events, each of which has a different numeric value. The numeric values are added together to determine a total score to predict risk of illness. The implication is that a greater number of major changes increase stress and the probability of illness. But it is significant to note that the death of a spouse has the highest weight.

The probability is high that most who have experienced the death of a spouse would testify that it is the most shattering, wrenching experience of their lives. Especially in the early stages of grief, too much additional change can be overwhelming. In an earlier chapter, I already mentioned that just after Dennis's death, I chose not to pursue the idea of quitting my job. Although in one way, quitting my job might have reduced stress, it would have been a huge change for me, on top of the huge change of Dennis's death. Change in itself, even positive change, can increase stress. The Holmes and Rahe scale includes events such as marriage, marital reconciliation, and retirement, along with negative events.

The death of a spouse is an enormous change in itself. It may also bring about many secondary changes that are involuntary. The loss of income from the spouse could be a major change. Income might be lost from the spouse's job, or from other sources. Social security allows for only one income to the survivor, although it is the larger of the two incomes.

Often a pension survivor benefit is only 50% of the full pension amount. These changes might result in further change, such as the necessity to sell possessions, move from one's house, or return to work.

There might be changes in friendships and relationships with relatives. Many widows/widowers discover their friends disappearing. In some cases, these are couples who were friends with the widow/widower and her/his spouse as a couple. Now perhaps they feel uncomfortable remaining friends with one person, the surviving member of the couple. Maybe they do not know how to interact with someone feeling such intense grief. Maybe the grief reminds them too intensely of what one of them will experience someday. Maybe they feel a threat to their own relationship somehow. The widow/widower is unlikely to know the reason why. These friends usually just disappear. Sometimes there are feuds with relatives. These events are all very, very painful to the widow/widower. These are changes on top of the death of the spouse, that add to the stress.

There will be other involuntary changes. The widow/widower will need to take over household responsibilities previously performed by the spouse, such as paying bills, filing taxes, making investment decisions, repairing household fixtures, cooking, or doing yard work. The widow/widower will need to sort through possessions of the spouse, and make decisions about selling, donating, or disposing of these things. The widow/widower might need to move, or change jobs.

Major decisions will need to be made, but now there might be no one to discuss these major decisions with, as once there was. This in itself is another big change. The isolation is a major change. Now there is no one with whom to eat meals. Even finding someone with whom to share a meal, and arranging the meeting, becomes a major task.

All these major changes are thrust upon the survivor, and add to the stress level. In addition to these involuntary changes, the survivor faces many choices for voluntary change. Does the survivor want to make a career change, start dating, move to a new location, sell some household goods, make investment changes, take in a renter? Grief counselors tend to advise those who have lost a spouse not to make any major life changes for at least a year, and possibly two years, after a spouse has died. The emotional turmoil of the loss could hamper decision-making capabilities. Also, the resulting change could add too much stress, on top of the major changes already contributing to the stress level.

If you are feeling overwhelmed with change, and feel the urge to avoid new responsibility, or are reluctant to make major life changes, this is probably a healthy urge. You should listen to your own intuition, and do only what you are ready to do and want to do. Do not let others bully you into giving away your spouse's possessions until you are ready to do so. Do not let others talk you into moving out of your house, or making major new investments, or volunteering for an organization, or starting to date, until and unless you are ready and are sure it's a good idea. Listen to the voice within. It knows what's best for your healing and your health.

John writes:

Death marks its domain by robbing the survivor of the opportunity to share day-to-day life with another. We miss their love, companionship, support, affirmation, and honesty. Death slammed the door shut! Sadly, death of a spouse bolsters lonesomeness. Growing old alone is a distinct and real possibility. Widowhood casts survivors into a murky quagmire.

On the upside, survivors, in their new reality, do not require permission to decide whether to do or not do something. I only have to deal with "What do I want to do now". The past seems shattered, but future hope abounds if one chooses to explore their newly found or rediscovered world.

New circumstances enable widowed survivors to recreate themselves to face and live within their new reality. Widowed survivors who have experienced the deepest levels of unconditional love and intimacy may never again be privy to this wonder, a once in a lifetime occurrence. In marriages where there was no deep love, affection, or mutual respect, survivors may process the loss differently, coldly, and dispassionately.

Deep unconditional love, hard to explain, is the vibrant connection between soul mates. Nothing can explain how two people's inner energy affects each other so deeply. Participants become committed, intertwined, and comfortable with each other. Their euphoria accounted for feeling invulnerable, taking their special bond for granted, and presuming nothing would ever change. Death plays no favorites and demolishes that perfect world. Widowed survivors realize nothing lasts forever!

Memories of both good and rough times stand in sharp contrast with each other. The widowed survivor may never again feel the passion, fire, or wholeness experienced in the life with their deceased mate. Your lost love completed you, fired the heart and soul of your being, and became your center core. This type of deep love is virtually unexplainable. This special love was a dynamic, living presence. Death of a spouse creates a devastating emptiness, a confounding abyss, and potentially a permanent void.

But death of a spouse does not exclude or eliminate the possibility of a survivor finding new love and companionship. Even if a survivor finds a new relationship or new love, no one can pretend the past never happened. The scar created by the death of a spouse remains forever. But the future is unscripted. Remain open to all possibilities. Hope abounds in a positive way to which many survivors can attest.

Many survivors have been smitten with the fairy tale happy-ever-after syndrome. Survivors need to grant themselves approval to carry on and be unafraid to love again after the death of their spouse. There is no transgression when survivors grant themselves personal permission to keep all possibilities and options open.

4.4 Widowed with Children vs. without Children

Kathy writes:

Dennis died only weeks before Thanksgiving and Christmas. In the early raw days of my grief, I desperately reached out to four different support groups. One morning at one such group, I was sitting in a circle of widows, when the coordinator went around the group and asked each of us how we were spending the upcoming holiday. Every single one replied that she or he was spending the time with children. When my turn came, I could say only that I didn't know how I would be spending the time.

I found that it was a painful moment, and increased my sense of isolation. Dennis and I had no children. But at each support group, so often the discussion would refer to children calling to check on the widow or widower, or to offer support or advice, or connection with grandchildren. I felt as if every other widow or widower had children for support except for me. And it seemed as if everyone else assumed that each of us had children. And so often, it made it difficult to make new friends with other widows and widowers, because each of them already had all their time consumed by involvement with their children.

I thought that my sense of the statistics must be exaggerated, so I looked up a few articles. I found that the number of childless older people is expected to increase between now and 2030. But childless older people are still in the minority; estimates range from 11.6% to 20% (Redfoot, Feinberg, and Houser, 2013; Zhang and Hayward, 2001). I am surprised that the percentage is that large, even though it is a minority. Zhang and Hayward cite research by Koropeckyj-Cox (1998), who suggested that childlessness might have more negative effects on widows than on married couples, divorced people, or those who were never married. Still-married childless couples tend to support each other's needs; divorced childless people experience less stress because childlessness results in fewer negotiations in the divorce process; never-married childless people are likely already to have formed long-term social networks. Childless widows used to be part of a couple who supported each other's needs, but now are thrust out into a world with no support.

I found an article by Kelley Lynn (2014) that so moved me that it evoked feelings I didn't realize I had until I encountered the article. (Refer to the "Resources" section.) She points out how the widowed community is geared towards people with children, and how alienated those of us who are childless can feel at certain points in the conversation. And she talks about pain triggers, and concerns that we have about who will take care of us in our old age. We thought we would always take care of each other. And for many childless widows, the loss of the spouse is a double loss, because it was also the loss of the dream of having children, a loss which is unacknowledged, which has no support groups.

Childless widows have their own set of issues that are different from those with children. Besides the question of who will take care of us in old age, there are questions about housing arrangements, estate planning, whom to assign power of attorney for financial affairs, and power of attorney for health care. The answers to these questions are much more subject to change, as one meets new friends, remarries, or establishes new living situations.

And without children, there might be no one with whom to discuss bigger decisions and end-of-life issues. We discussed these questions with our spouse, and now widows and widowers who have children might be able to discuss these questions with their children. But those of us who are childless widows must decide by ourselves, or must find close friends, or other relatives, who are willing to help serve as a sounding board.

Those who have children can have their own difficulties. Widows and widowers have told me stories about their children who were overly controlling. One widow told me about her son who did not permit her to invite a male friend to the first Thanksgiving dinner after her husband had died, eleven months before, even though she was hosting the Thanksgiving meal at her own house. She asked her son why not, and he replied that it had been less than a year. She answered, "That means I can invite him next month!" But she did comply with his wishes on that holiday. A widower I knew complained that his daughter was constantly calling him, too often. Adult children can make it very difficult for a widow/widower to form a new relationship. Children might have concerns about inheritance, or about their own place in a newly formed family, or they might be concerned about their parent's well-being.

Younger widows or widowers with young children at home have another unique set of issues. Now they must raise a child, or children, alone, which they may have never expected to do. They also must work with their child's own grief. The book *From Eulogy to Joy*, listed in the "Resources" section of this book, contains an interesting chapter on children's perspectives on death, revealed through their eyes.

There is always a road not travelled, an alternative decision that would have made our lives completely different. But ultimately each of us, with children or childless, must find our own way. We can help each other by being kind to each other, by noticing our differences as well as our commonalities, and accommodating each other.

John writes:

Some survivors have children and others are childless. These differences create separate scenarios.

Childless survivors may feel loneliness, depression, consternation, and emptiness. These heightened sensations reinforce the realization of "I'm an orphan now." The childless survivor, if fortunate, will have built a support system consisting of family, friends, a church community, neighbors, and others. The childless survivor may be forced to stand alone, be independent, and function with limited or no emotional support. They must rely on their personal initiative, ingenuity, determination, and relationships.

Childless survivors may isolate themselves, not wanting to impose on their support system. Personal pride, stubbornness, or hesitancy to reach out for help increases their vulnerability. The childless survivor may shun social connectivity because of not wanting to feel out of place in social settings. Many naturally struggle with "I do not want to be a tag along." Isolation becomes a convenient, easy, and safe harbor for survivors who lack the courage or motivation to get up, get out, and get moving.

Childless survivors respect the fact that members of their support network have busy personal lives. Survivors do not want to overburden others with their problems. Confusion and frustration rules what to do or not to do, giving the impression of "I really do not give a hoot"; "no one cares whether I live or die"; and "let the chips fall where they may".

There is also a tendency to neglect or not tend to vehicular or household maintenance matters and repairs. Such may only escalate problems and the potential for increased expenses in cases where a preventive maintenance program would have averted a potential household system breakdown. Some survivors do not know when or if a repair may be needed nor how to obtain assistance. They hesitate to ask.

The childless survivor's dilemma is complicated, awkward, and self-destructive. Hesitating to reach out for help in a timely manner can lead to unforeseen personal and financial difficulties. Thus the childless widowed survivor may feel they have no one to readily consult. The circumstance can be sad.

Discussions of holiday plans or vacations with childless survivors may conjure an uncomfortable situation laden with frustration, jealousy, and exasperation. Consider the following, perhaps not so uncommon scenario.

A survivor's family member or widowed friend with children says, "I'm having the grandchildren for a week over the holiday while their parents get away for a little vacation."

Another responds, "I'm going to my daughter's house for the holiday."

A third reports, "We're having a family gathering at the Shopping Center Restaurant party room. We have such a crowd that none of our homes can host everyone.   It'll be such fun!"

Then they ask the childless survivor "What are you doing for the holiday?"

"I don't know; probably nothing. I have no place to go. I may go to services, then home and watch a movie or take a nap. Maybe I'll send out for a pizza if any place is open, or defrost a TV dinner. I don't celebrate holidays anymore; one day is pretty much like the next." Sadly, the childless survivor may have few options. It's not uncommon for some of them to be sad, alone, apathetic, bitter, or unenthusiastic about holidays.

Childless widowed survivors can help themselves by reaching out if they do not want to be alone at holidays or other special times. They can gather with others, in similar circumstances, enjoy holiday times, and create new traditions.

After the deaths of our sons, Nancy and I celebrated holidays with friends who were also alone. We called our group the Holiday Orphans, created traditions and reasons to celebrate, and enjoyed having the time to be with others for the holiday. We gathered at a local restaurant, reconvened to someone's house to socialize, and later went home. This enriching ritual helped pass the holiday with friends, enhanced our ability to cope, and brightened our outlook. We proactively tried to avoid being alone for the holidays. As a couple, we participated until Nancy died. Since then, I generally prefer to meet with friends for a quiet meal and reflections on happier times. But I have avoided holiday celebrations, preferring to be alone; the decision was mine.

Breaking out of the self-woven "pity party" cocoon can be difficult but not impossible. Many widowed survivors have children. One might believe the course of a widowed survivor with children creates an easy path, when compared to the childless survivor.

Some widowed survivors with children or stepchildren may not have sustainable, friendly relationships with their offspring. At times families can become estranged after the death of a spouse.

The survivor with children often harbors the burden of keeping the family together. Unity and harmony are important, especially if surviving children are younger and still living at home. The survivor may end up being a single parent with a regular job. The widowed survivor with children may have to relearn how to budget and manage time more effectively to be where they are needed.

In cases where children are older, and possibly married, the survivor may become the focal point of family controversy for multiple reasons:

1. Who will take care of mom (dad)?
2. Who is going to support mom (dad)?
3. What if mom (dad) decides to move?
4. Can mom (dad) get on with no help? Will mom (dad) live here?
5. How will mom's (dad's) widowed status impact our lives?
6. Is mom (dad) always going to be hanging around or underfoot?
7. What are we supposed to do?

Unfortunately, some children with widowed parents become so overly enmeshed and concerned about what they anticipate might be required of them, that they forget to ask their widowed parent what they want, need, or plan to do. As a result of unspoken conversations and presumed expectations, some of the children hide out or become scarce, want to take over or dominate the survivor's life, or become resentful before they really know all of the details. The danger of presumption coupled with failure to hold meaningful dialog creates confusion, unnecessary stress, and unfortunate misunderstandings. Many adult children forget that their parents relish personal independence and freedom. Hence open and honest conversations should be proactively pursued to define potentials, resolve concerns, clarify assumptions, slay phantom dragons, share expectations, and agree on what is going to happen before making any changes. Everyone needs to be heard!

4.5 Nonstandard Circumstances of Grief

Kathy writes:

The death of a spouse is devastating, but there are sometimes circumstances that can make it even more difficult. These circumstances can cause the grieving survivor to wonder: Am I all alone? Am I the only one who has ever encountered such a painful situation, on top of the death itself? Can I survive this? You might have been asking yourself this question, or you might be wondering about the extreme difficulty endured by a widowed friend. If so, this chapter is especially for you.

These circumstances might relate to difficulties in the relationship with the one who has died, or they might be involved in the nature of the death itself, or they might have started after the death, during the grieving process. This chapter cannot include every possible situation, but includes examples and stories. You might discover commonalities with your own experience in these stories. The purpose of this chapter is, first of all, to acknowledge that these different circumstances exist. Not all stories are fairy tales. Just reading these stories may provide comfort, to find that you are not so alone. Secondly, you might find here some ideas for working through the overwhelming feelings resulting from these circumstances.

Imperfect Relationships

During one grief support group session I attended, a man came into the room accompanied by his daughter. He proceeded to tell us that he and his late wife had hated each other. He told us many stories about their arguments and interactions. But he was very confused about his feelings. At one point, he broke down in tears. The moderator said that he must have also loved her, or he would not be feeling such conflict. In most grief support groups, I heard only stories about great love and loss. This man must have heard the same kinds of stories, and must have felt so alone with his conflicting feelings. But he did find in our group people who listened and accepted him.

As human beings, none of us is perfect. Because we are imperfect, our relationships are likewise imperfect. All of us have gone through difficult periods in our relationship with our partner, no matter how compatible we might seem to each other and to the outside world. We have all said things to our partner that we would like to erase from our past, but we cannot. But some of us have more difficulties in our relationship than others. The relationship might have constantly teetered on the brink of divorce. The relationship might have been extremely dysfunctional, so that most interactions were laced with anger and hurt. When that partner dies, the survivor must deal with many conflicting feelings. A support group who listens and accepts can help. Somewhere there are others with similar experiences, and talking with them can help one feel less alone. Working with a grief therapist who understands these issues can also be very beneficial.

In another case, a woman revealed to our group that her husband had committed adultery a few years before his death. He had told her that he was in love with the other woman and planned to leave. The affair lasted several months and was extremely painful. Eventually he left the affair, and the couple had just started to reconcile when he died suddenly. Now she was flooded with the pain of recognition that their relationship, that they had just started to rekindle, had been suddenly cut off. When she came to our group, this woman told us that she had felt so alone, with her story, unlike the other stories. But finding others with similar stories helped her to feel less alone, and to begin healing the pain.

Someone reported the story of a woman who discovered *after* her husband's death that he had been having an affair. At that point, there was no chance to talk or to reconcile. The discovery negatively affected her feelings towards her late husband, and greatly increased the difficulty of working through the loss. The films *The Descendants* and *About Schmidt*, mentioned in the "Resources" section, both deal with this theme of discovery of betrayal after the death of a partner.

No one else in the group had experienced either of these exact situations, but another woman reported that before her late husband was diagnosed with cancer, they had a major fight about his refusal to seek health care. She didn't speak to him for weeks and considered leaving him. Then he was diagnosed, and they had four months before his death when they were able to talk through their conflict and reconcile. She was able to explain that her anger had come from love, and from fear about his health. She still felt guilt about her earlier behavior, but was grateful for the reconciliation. She found some relief after his death by writing in a journal about her anger, and writing a letter to him to ask for forgiveness. She offered these coping ideas to the others in the group, and suggested to the newcomers that this grief support group would be a safe place to express all emotions, positive and negative.

Feelings of guilt are very common. Many of us spend time and energy considering what we could have, or should have done. But it can do us no good to consider the past. We cannot change what has already happened, but can change only the future. Often it is ourselves that we need to forgive, more than others.

In this life, a partnership with another human being is necessarily imperfect. Especially in a long relationship, there are inevitably times of conflict and pain, along with other times of connection and bliss. During the raw time immediately following the death of a partner, there may be a tendency to focus on regret, remorse, and guilt. Over time, these feelings tend to melt away, and the essential love remains. Sometimes a good grief therapist can help the survivor work through these feelings.

Traumatic Death

Death itself is traumatic to those left behind. But there are circumstances that add to the trauma, such as suicide, war, crime, or accidental death. There are entire books, organizations, and grief support groups that specialize in help with surviving the aftermath of these experiences.

The "Resources" section of this book includes references to web resources, support groups, and books that may help. There is a special list in the "Resources" section of websites dedicated to those who have lost someone to suicide, and another special list of websites dedicated to those who have lost someone to homicide. The main list of websites contains a link to the American Widow Project website, for military widows. That organization also maintains a hotline. The book *Wave* describes the traumatic loss of a woman's entire family to a tsunami, and the book *Radical Survivor* describes the loss of another woman's entire family in a plane crash. These books are also listed in the "Resources" section.

Difficult Times during Grieving

One widow I know was disowned by her partner's family right after her partner's death. Similarly, another widow arrived at our grief support meeting in torment, because her partner's family had opposed their union from the start. She and her fiancé had not yet married, so the family was able to block her from even attending his funeral. Of course, this adversity further increased the suffering of the respective grieving partners. They needed the support of others even more than they otherwise would have, so they wisely reached out to our support groups.

In some cases, difficult existing relationships increase the suffering of widows, but in other cases, new relationships can add to the pain. The moderator at one of our grief support groups told the story of a widow who met and married someone only months after the death of her husband. Apparently her first marriage had been a good one, but she was very lonely and chose someone before she could have known him well. At first she felt infatuated with her new love, and her pain of loss faded somewhat. But soon he became physically abusive. She found herself in the position of having to heal both from the wrenching event of her husband's death, and from the searing eruptions in this new relationship. The pain was nearly more than she could bear sometimes. She could find no other widows with similar experiences who could completely understand, so she found herself attending two different kinds of support groups. Eventually she escaped the abuse, but was deeply traumatized, and had to work through the healing process for a long time.

Suggestions

When my own husband died, I told a friend that there were many things that I wished I could say to my husband, but of course I could not talk to him now. But my friend suggested that I try doing just that. So I tried talking to my late husband even though he wasn't physically present, and it does seem to help. You can say all the things that you wish you had said, or had time to say, even now. Talking to your loved one can't do any harm, and if they can hear you, then they will know. Talking also can help to open yourself to listen to your loved one as well. Sometimes talking to the one you lost can result in profound experiences of communication that are very healing.

There are also useful exercises for letting go of negative feelings. For example, a practice called The Sedona Method focuses on how to release feelings. There are many meditation practices that can provide comfort. Refer to the "Resources" section of this book. That section includes a reference to a book about the Sedona Method. That section also refers to a book entitled *From Eulogy to Joy,* which includes chapters on the death of someone whom you hate or with whom you are angry; deaths by murder, suicide, and accidents; the perspectives of children on death; and many other nonstandard circumstances surrounding the death of a loved one.

John writes:

When unusual circumstances surrounding a death occur, the widowed spouse may first need to bring closure to the death experience and related circumstances. (See Chapter 1.3: "Physical and Emotional Sensations" and Chapter 3.4: "Grieving Styles".)

Several examples come to mind. I know the story of an individual whose spouse died overseas. When he received news of her death, his primary task, to achieve closure, was the retrieval and the return home of her remains. During the immediate time period following her death, he described turning on "automatic pilot" to accomplish his objective. He became task oriented, cold, detached, and impersonal.

He stated there was no time to grieve or mourn. His full time job was to retrieve her body rapidly and without any distraction. Traveling to the country where she died, he quickly discovered the complex maze of regulations pertaining to claiming her remains. The morass of requirements, codes, regulations, logistics, and expenses were overwhelming. He described the project as arduous, contentious, cumbersome, and confusing. He sought help from the US Embassy.

Once his task was completed, approximately six weeks later, he donned the mantle of bereavement and mourning.

Similar circumstances occur when death results from war. Casualties of war are real. A widowed military survivor may not fully accept nor comprehend the death of a spouse, especially one who was deployed. Many have stated "I hoped they were wrong; then I saw the body." They, the survivor, actually needed to see the body, confirming their beloved was really dead, before they could accept the reality of the death and begin mourning. Survivors grasp for a last glimmer of hope or the lingering shadow of a doubt which causes a "let's wait and see" posture. Sometimes complications arise. In some circumstances, the casket is permanently sealed before shipping because the condition of the body is so horrid that a viewing is deemed unadvisable.

The same occurs when the deceased donates their body to medical science. The remains may eventually be returned to the family for final disposition, but customarily they are cremated and disposed of by the educational institution. This situation delays final arrangements for an extended period of time. In the end, there may be no funeral but rather a memorial service. Such may force the bereaved spouse into a non-standard or delayed mode of grieving. Unfortunately for some survivors, there is no closure until the memorial service has transpired.

Grief may be dulled when the marital relationship was domestically violent, abusive, unloving, or volatile. In these cases, the surviving spouse may experience the sense of loss along with relief, safety, and peace knowing the ordeal is over. I heard a surviving spouse of such a relationship remark "I'm glad he (she) is dead. I don't have to worry about whom he (she) may hurt. I no longer have to be concerned about the prospect of him (her) committing self-harm. I no longer have to fear for my life, or others', for personal safety, or well-being. I'm glad it's over."

Completing and closing unfinished business remains an essential component to remedy nonstandard circumstances of grief. Sometimes "unfinished business" is driven by external forces beyond the control of the survivor. A great primary example was mentioned in the story above, where the husband wanted to bring his wife's body home but was prevented from doing so immediately due to cumbersome, complicated regulations. He was cast into the wait-and-see mode until all legal requirements were met. Hence survivors cannot begin grieving until they receive the "all clear" signal in these special situations.

4.6 Customs, Traditions, and Expectations

Kathy writes:

In the 19th century in the United States and parts of Europe, a formal set of rules for mourning had developed. Widows wore black heavy clothing, black veils, and sometimes jewelry made of jet, for up to four years after the death. There were rules about the timeframes for introducing conventional clothing again. Later the rules relaxed so that the clothing was required for a year.

By the late twentieth century, black attire was worn mainly at the funeral itself. Formal mourning customs have greatly relaxed, but there are still a few remnants of older traditions. Sunglasses sometimes replace veils to conceal evidence of weeping. Sometimes black jet jewelry is still worn.

But choices have become more individualized. Debates can be found on widow/widowers' forums about what to do about the wedding ring. Some leave it on the left ring finger for many months. Others move it to the right ring finger. Still others remove it after a time. Some hang it on a chain around the neck. A widow I met many years ago bought herself a new ring with many colored stones that she considered a widow's ring.

There is also increasing recognition that the timeframe for grief is highly individual. There is still some cultural expectation that the period will last at least a year, or perhaps two years. But some widows/widowers begin dating only a few months after the death of the spouse, and some remarry very quickly. Some survivors find that they need to seek companionship even at the same time that they mourn the loss of their spouse. Some people accept this, and others pass judgment. In the early stages after the loss, a new companion can be especially difficult for children to accept.

Conversely, some choose a longer period of mourning, and some choose never to date or remarry at all. Sometimes others have issues with this as well, and urge the widow/widower to "move on". These expectations can be stressful for the widow/widower, who is the only person in a position to know the best course of action and the best timing.

Only the one who suffered the loss knows how best to proceed with his/her own life. Only that person knows all the details of his or her own experience, and of all the factors involved, to be able to make the best decision. Others who have not experienced exactly what the survivor has experienced, even other survivors, are not in a position to pass judgment or tell that person what to do. The role of family and friends is to listen and support.

John writes:

Accepted contemporary social conventions can conflict with time-honored, family-centered tenets, time-honored cultural values, and religious beliefs. Sometimes the conflicts are difficult to separate, interpret, or comprehend. Variations and exceptions are too numerous to mention, as each will produce its own unique points of contention.

When my grandfather died, over 60 years ago, acceptable cultural traditions warranted dressing in black for funeral-related events and activities. We spent three days at the funeral home receiving mourners. On the third day, we caravanned from the funeral home to church for the funeral mass, drove to the cemetery for burial, then back to the house for a reception.

Afterwards, Grandma wore black until she died. Mom wore black for one year. We sent no holiday cards that year. Holiday celebrations were minimal. The same traditions were observed when other family members died. My ancestors emigrated from Western Europe. People of other cultures follow and observe their respective rituals, traditions, and customs.

Remember the earlier example of funeral observances in the New Orleans French Quarter? (See Chapter 2.1: "The Funeral/Memorial Service".) The funeral ceremony celebrates the life of the deceased with festive dancing and music, coupled with mourning rituals. Society's perceptions of funeral rites, customs, and tradition are changing.

Some cultural rituals stipulate burial should take place as quickly as possible. Some do not permit autopsies, embalming, or cremation, unless required by law, and others do. Importantly the culturally driven rituals of everyone should be respected as much as possible. All peoples, regardless of national origin, race, culture, or creed, celebrate at the birth of a new baby, dance at weddings, and cry at funerals.

4.7 Coping With Those Who Say or Do the Wrong Thing

Kathy writes:

"I know what it's like." I looked at my never-married friend. "You know what it's like to lose a spouse?" "I lost my father," she said. I had to explain that it was a different kind of experience to lose a spouse. I lost both of my parents before I lost my husband, so I knew just how different it was. I found it very painful to lose my parents, whom I had known my whole life, who had cared for me as a child, and for whom I had acted as caregiver in their last days. But my husband was someone with whom I shared the deepest intimacy, my closest confidant, my best friend, who was there with me when I slept at night, who shared every day with me, and with whom I had hoped to share the rest of my life. I felt that half of me had been ripped away. The loss of my husband was very, very different from the loss of a parent.

Another one exclaimed, "It's been five years! You should get rid of these things!" and proceeded to stack them up to remove them. I had to explain that this was my decision, that only I was in a position to know what to do with things left behind, and when to do it.

Some were judgmental about the grieving process. One friend said I was holding on too much by grieving; another claimed it was an act of self-pity. I had to explain that grieving is a process of releasing, of letting go, of growing, of finding my new place, of reaching out to others in a spirit of love and compassion.

I knew that someone who had not walked in my shoes had no right to tell me what to do, not even another widow. I knew that I needed to grieve in my own way, and in my own timeline. I knew that I deserved not to be judged and criticized, but to be supported, by those who say they are my friends.

Then I discovered The Mourner's Bill of Rights, developed by Alan Wolfelt. It's an assertion of ten rights of those who mourn. Refer to the "Resources" section of this book for the website where one can obtain the list. I have printed out The Mourner's Bill of Rights, and sometimes show it to anyone who begins to tread on my rights.

Especially in the beginning, a question about the cause of my husband's death was an extremely painful question. I had not asked for an autopsy, so the answer was unclear. Also, the question evoked flashbacks to that excruciating event that I did not want to relive. My reaction to the question was to experience pain, but I felt the pain was unintended, so I tried to answer the questions anyway.

Sometimes people are thoughtless and judgmental, but at other times, it is inexperience that results in painful comments. There are those people who genuinely want to provide solace, but do not know what to say. Honesty, humility, and empathy are the most helpful traits. If you have not experienced the loss of a partner, you can just admit that you do not know what it is like, but that you imagine it must be incredibly difficult. Allow the person grieving to talk, and follow their lead. Do not judge. Do not give advice. Do not tell them what to do. Just offer them the opportunity to talk, but only if they wish to. Just listening is a valuable service. Ask if there is any practical task you can help with. Do not abandon them. Forgive them if they are very self-absorbed right now. This is a time when surviving is all they can do. The "Resources" section of this book includes a list of websites and articles for friends of widows that provide much insight and more details.

If you are the widow listening to comments that are irritating or painful, then you will need to decide how you wish to deal with them. I try to be patient with those who seem well intentioned, especially if they are good friends. Sometimes it's necessary to be firm, or even show anger, especially if they are violating my boundaries. Of course it depends on the situation. There is a very good story in the book *Companion Through the Darkness*, by Stephanie Ericsson. Stephanie is dining with two friends, both still married to live partners. One friend pushes Stephanie to "get over" it, and the other philosophizes that we are all alone anyway. Stephanie blows up and very eloquently tells her friends exactly what she thinks. This might not always be the best way to behave, but it surely feels good to read about it. This story reminded me of a time when I was with a group of still-married close friends, when they all started boasting about their anniversaries and how long they had been married. No one stopped to imagine how I might be feeling. I said nothing, but later I realized how I felt, and thought about what I might say if it happened again.

Hopefully our friends will forgive us, and realize that we are going through a period when it is all we can do to take care of our own needs, which are powerful right now, especially in the beginning. During this time, we become teachers about what is most important, because that is all that we can focus on now. Someday, we may be able to help our friends when they suffer loss. Because half of every couple will eventually become a widow or a widower. Each of us should show as much compassion to each other as we can.

John writes:

Some survivors realize that family and friends who have not experienced the death of a spouse may make illogical, foolish, or insensitive comments. Survivors may wonder why some made a particular comment that seemed totally out of nowhere or inappropriate. In some of these cases, survivors might have been just as happy if the uninformed source maintained their silence. Most remarks are intended to be comforting, not malicious, but some are foolish, irksome, and irrelevant.

Some comments I have heard include, but are not limited to:

<u>"Well it's God's will."</u> *Really, did God tell you? Do you have a special connection with the Almighty or some insight into the afterlife? Who told you?*

<u>"They're in a better place."</u> *How do you know? Did you visit? Did you see their new place? Did they telephone, text, write, or send a "wish you were here post card"? Did you ask how they enjoyed the trip? Do they live in a nice neighborhood?*

<u>"Aren't you over it yet?"</u> *Quick answer...*<u>*"Heck no!*</u> *I may never recover. Regretfully, when it happens to you (and it well may), then you'll understand my pain!"* (We really do not wish others to experience this pain.)

<u>"You need to get on with your life."</u> *I know what I have to do. Unless you've walked in my shoes please do not try to tell me what I need to do. Saying nothing would be better. Hug me. Take my hand. Let me know you are there. Your love, support and friendship are what I really need right now. Thanks for caring.*

<u>"Time will heal, you're hurt."</u> *I know you are trying to help and I hope you are right. But right now I feel hopeless, lost, empty, and sad. I can't see beyond my nose.*

<u>"Eventually you'll forget!"</u> *I do not ever want to forget! She was my light, my life, my love, and my soul mate. I pray you never have to walk this path, but unfortunately you might. I know if you ever do, you won't want to forget either.*

<u>"It must be so hard."</u> *You are totally correct. Yes, it is very hard. I appreciate your kind and gentle thoughts, comments, and empathy. Pardon my gruffness, if I overreact. This is the hardest thing I have ever had to deal with or face.*

"I know how you feel; my dog was hit by a car." *Sorry, not really the same. I know you mean well. Pets are precious companions who bring us a lot of happiness. Losing a pet hurts and can cause quite an emotional stir. But losing a pet, in my opinion, cannot remotely compare to the death of a spouse.*

"I share your sadness and know how you are hurting, I felt that way when my grandma died." *I too have been saddened by the loss of family and relatives. But my spouse was the love of my life. We were one, a team, a family...soul mates. Grandma was a wonderful part of our lives and we loved her very much. But it's just not the same. Thank you for sharing.*

"There are better days ahead." *I hope so and thanks for sharing your optimism.*

"Pray that the Good Lord will heal your hurt. I'm praying for you." *Thank you for being so thoughtful. Sometimes I question whether God is really listening or cares. I try to pray when I feel like it. Sometimes I ask, "Lord, where are you? I really need you now! Help me make sense out of this travesty. Hello, are you there...?"*

"Well it was just his (her) time." *Do you have access to people's timeline? What inside track makes you privy to all of this insider information? None of us will exit this life alive. No one lives forever. Your comment is not very helpful right now; in fact it seems hurtful. I am well aware of the facts of life.*

"Well it's for the best!" *But no, it's not, at least not for me. Maybe it's for the best because his (her) suffering is over. My spouse is dead and I'm alone! If your spouse dies, tell me how you feel. What makes you such an authority? This is easy for you to say; you really don't know, do you? Frankly, I hope you never have to know.*

<u>"God never gives you more than you can handle!"</u> *Once upon a time, I would have really been offended by this comment. But I have thought and reflected on this point. Today, right now, I'm here with you and we're talking. You are absolutely right; I got up this morning…how about that? But I may not feel this way tomorrow.*

Discussions within this chapter reinforce some things already known to survivors. Frequently those who have suffered the loss of a spouse speak too quickly before thinking. I recommend survivors be tolerant, understanding, and forgiving toward the apparent ignorance and insensitivity exhibited by inexperienced observers. Remember many "non-experiencers" may not really understand; there's no way they can. One may want to take the well-meaning pundit aside and gently advise them of how the thought behind their remark was appreciated but totally inappropriate. At the same time, ask them not to utter the same foolish comment again if they encounter a similar situation.

Share with them how much you appreciated:
- Being hugged;
- Their support, presence, warmth, and affirmation; and,
- Their acknowledgement of your grief by their comments: "I'm sorry for your loss"; "Call me if you want or need to talk. I'm here for you"; "I'll be praying for you"; "I'm sad with you"; "I love you".

Remember no one can have enough friends.

4.8 Getting Help

Kathy writes:

When the funeral was over, after everyone had left town and returned home, that is when I had to confront the isolation, silence, and intense waves of grief. That is when I needed to get help. Those things that helped me the most were the daily phone calls I received from a family member and from a friend, weekly visits with a grief therapist, and grief support groups. If someone offers to help, and you know you need it, it's good to accept that help.

For some people, accepting help is not easy. A previous chapter of this book presents the concept of grieving styles, and the idea that people grieve in different ways. You will need to find what works for you. However, if you sense that someone or something can help, ask for it, or seek it out. Those who offer to help want to be of service. You will be helping them by accepting their help.

I found grief support groups to be wonderful. Choosing a compatible support group is important. Some groups are generic grief support groups, not just for widows and widowers. They serve anyone grieving a loss, including relatives and friends, and sometimes include those who have divorced. However, I found it best to join the groups that focus on those whose partners have died. Other losses are very different, and it's too easy to lose time and perspective on those issues that do not help you. Right now, you need to focus on helping yourself.

Other widows are the only people who really understand what you are going through, because they themselves are going through it also. To hear others validate your emotions and reactions, and let you know you are not alone, is so valuable.

You might find yourself comparing notes, and getting new ideas for coping. In my experience, these groups are always very supportive and accepting. You might make new friends. In one group, when one of the widows found out I might be alone on Thanksgiving, she invited me to her house. I had only just met her.

In the beginning, I attended four different support groups. I needed all the support I could get. Some groups meet only once a month. One group met once a week, and also held activities on two or more additional days every week. I found that group most worthwhile.

Some people might need a more private expression of grief, rather than support groups. Grief therapy allowed me to focus exclusively on my own grief for an hour, and to share more private thoughts than in the groups. Also, I worked with a trained psychologist. Most of the support groups were led by another widow without professional credentials. I found value in both the groups and the individual therapy sessions. However, each survivor is different, and must choose what works for him or her.

If you find that you need help with finances, legal matters, raking your leaves, or eating enough food, reach out to others. If there are others who have already offered to help, contact them. They want to help, and you will be serving them by allowing them to do it. If you belong to a church, contact someone there. Contact a social services organization. Or ask your neighbors. Or find a professional whom you can hire.

Turn to the section at the back of this book entitled "Resources". Read through it and think to yourself what information you can use from it to get help for yourself. Think about what those who love you, or who have loved you, would want for you. Now is when you need help, and you deserve it.

John writes:

There seems to be a plethora of widowed survivor support groups. Some are community based, church sponsored, or professionally facilitated. These groups fulfill a multitude of purposes, cover a wide variety of agendas, and cater to different segments of the widowed population. The internet has several chat rooms that provide support for widowed survivors. No widowed spouse needs to be alone. One only needs to be open to asking for help and willing to clasp a friendly hand.

Many bereaved, traversing the path of their grief journey, have paid steep dues to belong to the Widowed Survivors' Club. No one joined voluntarily. Eligibility for membership is open to anyone who is widowed, much to our and their chagrin.

One displays courage to walk across the threshold and initially enter a support group meeting, class, or assembly. A standard greeting may be "We're sorry you're here, but we're glad you found us." Comfort, trust, and acceptance are readily apparent. No one judges the newcomer or questions their reason for attending. Group members already know instinctively. Newcomers are welcomed immediately and with open arms.

Emotional pains, stress, physical hurt, mental anguish, and spiritual questioning cover the broad spectrum of issues plaguing survivors. As stated previously, the four dimensions of the human psyche overlap and seamlessly interconnect. Since the dimensions seem to be interwoven, making it difficult to determine where one begins and ends, the issues dot the landscape.

Help is available. Some find solace through affiliation or attendance at gatherings of widowed support groups. Women generally outnumber men in these groups. The trend seems to be changing, as men seem to be receptive to reaching out for help and support.

All widowed survivors are "vulnerable prey" and casualties of grief, mourning, and bereavement. Longer-term members of support groups may offer each other and the newly widowed mutual insights and tips for moving ahead.

It's ok to reach out for help. Doing so reflects a step toward healing. Members of widowed support groups consist of people who comprehend the immeasurable, detrimental impact of widowhood. Support group members lend credible testimony to the enduring, scarring, and frequently permanent pains of widowhood.

Support group sponsors may be hospices, hospitals, funeral homes, churches, temples, synagogues, agencies, and volunteer groups, to name a few. Survivors are encouraged to search the internet, phone book, and other community resource bulletin boards to learn of support groups in their locale.

Some support groups offer pre-scripted, curriculum-based, content-oriented courses over a fixed period of time. Classes end when the assigned material is finished. Participants generally praise the multi-functional sharing, educational, informative, and supportive benefits of these groups. Grief, bereavement, and mourning are well covered. Sometimes the participants' needs for social contact remain unfulfilled, as the meeting agenda is preplanned. However, some groups modify the agenda to discuss matters of concern to group members, should the need arise. In some of these groups, members may gather informally after meetings to socialize and support each other. Each survivor should choose and explore the forums, groups, and avenues that are most beneficial and available to them personally.

Groups utilizing facilitators who have experienced the death of a spouse are extremely beneficial. Participants effectively benefit from the instructors' knowledge, expertise, and background. However when the facilitator is not an aggrieved spouse, overall group effectiveness may be blunted. In my estimation, group facilitators who are not experiencers cannot fully comprehend the pain or emotional plight of the widowed survivor.

Some groups provide social and recreational support for survivors. These groups schedule regular periodic meetings and social events. Members can participate at their discretion and their comfort level. Some befriend each other and interact socially. Some members have even remarried.

Support groups may offer input, respite, social connection, and a safe haven for survivors to cry and/or be with others who understand. No member is considered a stranger in these circles. The common threads binding these groups are experience, trust, hospitality, acceptance, and support.

4.9 Healing through Introspection

Kathy writes:

Introspection means to look within. Introspection is the process of observing, and sometimes recording, one's own thoughts and emotional processes. Introspection is an active thinking process in which one analyzes one's own thoughts, to trace them back to their origins, to get a deeper understanding of oneself.

Introspection is different from meditation. In meditation, we focus on the present moment, our experience right now, and rest the mind from thinking. When thoughts do arise, we observe them, without attaching to them. In introspection, we analyze and explore thoughts; in meditation, we just witness thoughts. Introspection gives us insight into ourselves, and why we do what we do. Meditation gives us connection with reality as it exists here and now. Ultimately it can give us experience of the divine.

Both introspection and meditation can help those who are grieving to facilitate their own healing process. Meditation can help with releasing the intense emotions associated with grief. In meditation, a grieving person would observe the emotions, and then let them pass. To let the emotions pass, first one must allow oneself to experience fully the grief, in all its physical and emotional manifestations. Avoiding or suppressing the emotions of grief just postpones the healing process. Meditation also helps the grieving person find connection and reach groundedness by focus on present experience.

With introspection, one examines the emotions of grief, and the memories leading up to the loss, and one questions past experiences and beliefs. This can result in new insight and growth.

Many forms of psychotherapy serve as guided introspection. The therapist encourages the client to examine and to question their own thoughts, feelings, and behavior, in order to form new insights. Some people find it helpful to write down their introspective thoughts in a journal. The act of writing seems to facilitate the thought process. And it becomes possible to re-read what one has written, and form new insights. Some use prayer as a form of introspection.

Everyone grieves differently, but many people find healing by turning within. I have been meditating for many decades, and find it to be an essential part of my life. I also use introspection, in my thoughts, my writing, and in therapy with my grief counselor. There are many books, workshops, and guides for learning the most useful methods. Stang (2014) has written a book containing guided meditation exercises specifically designed for grief. Refer to the "Resources" chapter of this book. A session with a grief counselor might be the best way to learn how to use introspection for the grief process.

John writes:

The term "introspection" tends to confuse many people. To some, introspection may mean entering a state of deep meditative self-reflection. For some this description may be correct. Other individuals practice meditation, yoga, discernment, and contemplative prayer.

Introspection enables individuals to deeply reflect on their innermost ideas, images, feelings, thoughts, ambitions, attitudes, and emotions by retreating into their personal central core.

Many civilizations, worldwide, espouse the benefits of introspection and meditation. Some practitioners of the healing arts and holistic medicine cite the positive effects of introspection to curative and healing processes.

Some survivors practice introspection and meditation in their daily spiritual lives, endeavoring to connect with their deeper inner self. Many rely on introspection to heighten personal awareness of current situations, surroundings, and state of life.

Introspection allots personal time for self-reflection, contemplation, thinking, analysis, and assessment. Those who engage in introspection may prefer to spend solitary time in silence, away from others. Others may find inner peace in the practice of yoga, prayer, discernment, or guided meditation.

After the death of a spouse, once the hubbub of activities related to funerals, settling estates, and figuring out how to get on with life subside, the widowed survivor may welcome a hiatus for solitude, quiet time, and reflective introspection to begin to grasp their "new" reality. The practice of introspective exercises may help a survivor release guilt, grief, and sadness. However, the pause is temporary, and eventually the survivor's inner being will clamor for companionship, socialization, and human contact.

Questions, thoughts, or concerns related to "What could I have done differently?" "Her death is my fault"… taking guilt trips or assigning personal blame may be excellent focal points for reflection. Introspection provides the opportunities to examine what really happened, and may help one develop a clearer mental picture of their new reality.

Introspection involves "me" looking into and at "myself", no one else. I can be truthful to myself and acknowledge my guilt or innocence with candid honesty and without fear of being judged. I have nothing to hide. I can realize inner peace and face my new future with courage, conviction, and hope.

I have developed ***A Guide to Personal Healing***, a series of questions a widowed survivor may wish to review when pursuing introspection or self-healing. The guide is designed to facilitate personal healing.

All can benefit from a holistic approach to personal healing. The process can commence through the practices of private and personal introspection as well as by "Healing through Writing", discussed in Chapter 4.10.

The concepts of unconditional love, forgiveness, honesty, and prayer were the core values upon which Bishop Robert H. Mize founded St. Francis Boys' Homes in the 1940s. (I was chief operating officer of this national, multi-corporate organization for many years.)

These precepts have become very important to me in both my private and professional lives. These core values embody precepts that are pertinent to discussions, up to this point.

1. **Unconditional Love**
   - What is unconditional love?
   - How can I give unconditional love?
   - How do I receive unconditional love?
   - How do I know unconditional love?
   - Have I ever practiced unconditional love?
   - How can I demonstrate unconditional love?

2. **Forgiveness is the Greatest Instrument of Personal Self-transformation and Introspection**
   - What is personal self-transformation and introspection?
   - Do I need forgiveness?
   - Do I want forgiveness?
   - Do I want to practice forgiveness?

- What's the difference between forgetting and forgiving?
- What are the similarities between forgetting and forgiving?
- How do forgetting and forgiving relate to self-transformation, inner healing, and personal introspection?
- Why do I want to think about forgetting, forgiveness, self-transformation, and personal introspection?
- Is there anyone who makes my day turn to night that could benefit from me forgetting and forgiving?
- How can forgetting and forgiving help me physically, mentally, spiritually, and emotionally?

3. **Honesty and Frankness in Accepting the Accountabilities, Rewards, and Consequences of Personal Actions**
- Whom am I fooling?
- I'm never wrong, am I?
- They started it, didn't they?
- What do I have to be accountable for?
- Is it always right to be right?
- Do I dare be honest with myself?
- Do I want to be honest with myself?
- What are the risks?
- Will I still respect myself in the morning?
- How do I accept and acknowledge the accountabilities, rewards, and consequences resulting from my actions?
- How does it benefit me to say, "Gee you might be right and I might be wrong?"
- Does my sense of personal pride prevent me from admitting I could be wrong?
- What are the risks?
- Do I write, meditate, pray, talk, or communicate with an accountability partner?

4. **Start and End Each Day with God**
- Do I have a God?

- Do I know God? It's been said God is dead.
- Where is God in my times of sadness, desolation, and need?
- How is our relationship?
- Whom am I kidding?
- Does God really care about me?
- Do I have room in my life for God?
- Do I have the time?
- Am I willing to make the time?
- Did I take time in the past?
- What caused me to break stride?
- How do I start?
- Will it hurt?
- Why me?
- Now what?
- How do I make the first move?
- Do I examine my life periodically in light of these precepts?

The questions mentioned in ***A Guide to Personal Healing*** can be used in many situations. I believe it to be in the best interest of each individual to take time to carefully take stock of any situation before making a final commitment or a major decision. The following lists some situations in which reflecting on the Guide may be helpful.

When one struggles with the shock and regrets encountered at the death of a spouse, the Guide can provide a framework for personal reflection and introspective thought.

When one grapples with a decision about making a potential major life change, questions in the Guide can help them assess potential positive and negative impacts of a possible course of action.

If one contemplates entering a more serious relationship, with a new significant other, the Guide can assist them in formulating their thought processes, alternatives, and directions in which to proceed.

In each of the previously cited situations, the survivor is solely responsible for their decisions. This is an exciting opportunity for many because they gain the freedom to try new things, travel, and explore new pursuits. However, while the Guide cannot make the final decision, survivors can use it as a reflective tool to analyze the pros and cons of their thought processes. Final decisions rest with the individual survivor.

4.10 Healing through Writing

Kathy writes:

The grieving survivor can heal through writing in much the same way as he or she can heal through introspection, as presented in the previous chapter. When one writes about one's own grieving process, one tends to write introspectively, by observing, analyzing, and recording one's own thoughts and emotions, and gaining new insights. But there is something different about doing this in writing, as opposed to just thinking to oneself.

First of all, the process of verbalizing in writing helps to clarify one's thoughts. Writing down a description of one's thoughts and feelings in a clear, communicative way demands that the writer think even more deeply about the subject, with more precision. Sometimes the process also evokes thoughts and feelings that the writer did not know were there. The process prompts the writer to re-read what was just written before adding the next sentence, which slows down the thought process and deepens it. New startling insights might emerge at that point in time.

Secondly, writing out one's feelings can provide an emotional release that is very healing. Writing might be the only mechanism available for releasing feelings that might otherwise be bottled up.

Thirdly, the writer can later return and re-read the material in all its detail. Memory limits the detail of what one can recall of a previous introspection if it is not in writing. Sometimes when one re-reads what has been written earlier, patterns might appear that were not apparent before, or other new insights might surface.

Fourthly, the writer can choose to publish the written material in a book or a blog. Other people can read it and react to it, resulting in still more insights. Then healing can take place for many people.

When I write about an interaction with someone, sometimes I find it useful to write it very objectively, as if I were a news reporter outside myself describing everything that happened. In this case, instead of writing introspectively, I leave out any description of my own interpretations or my emotions. Then when I go back and re-read it later, sometimes I find more empathy for the other person's point of view. Or sometimes it becomes more clear that I need to take a particular action. Sometimes I see aspects of the situation I didn't see while in the conversation. I write down my conclusions about what seems to be going on. Sometimes I can use the words I have written in a later conversation.

Some people find it easier to handwrite their thoughts in a diary or journal. Bookstores often sell blank books with attractive covers for diaries or journals. Writing might feel like a more creative process if the text is handwritten. On the other hand, if the text is typed into a word processor on a computer, then editing the text later becomes much easier. This is especially valuable if the text will become part of a blog or a published book, when the capability of a word processor to transfer and rearrange text can save a great deal of time and effort.

The best way to start is simply to start. Don't judge yourself harshly. Just begin to write whatever comes to mind. You can always edit later. No one else ever needs to read your journal unless you give permission. Set a reasonable schedule, allowing 20 or 30 minutes a day. Many people find that keeping a journal reduces stress, clarifies thinking, provides emotional release, produces better decisions, improves communication, and facilitates the healing process.

After Dennis died, one of my most powerful feelings was the urge to memorialize him, always to remember him. I wrote his obituary, and then expanded it later into a longer account of the story of our lives together. My journal is private, for now. My own parents wrote their memoirs, and they used those memoirs in later life as memory aids when they developed age-related memory loss. They also passed the memoirs down to their children and grandchildren. For survivors of loss, journals and memoirs can help preserve the memory of those we loved.

John writes:

Through writing, I keep Nancy's memory and legacy alive. I want to tell our story and remember her. The world needs to know who she was, what she did, and that she made a difference. As a spouse, parent, grandmother, daughter, teacher, friend, advocate, and neighbor she touched and influenced many lives in a very positive way. The idea of healing through writing may help others hone their coping skills and soothe their wounds. To reiterate a previous point...every survivor has a story to tell. No matter how far along any survivor is on the grief journey path, each has an abundance of knowledge to share and a huge capacity to continue learning. Each survivor can help others to learn, develop, and enhance their coping skills by setting a personal example.

Writing documents the personal story of the individual survivor and their deceased spouse. Writing provides a cathartic outlet and a powerful means to record the details of an individual grief journey and the life behind after the death of a spouse. The newly widowed are searching for their new normal and trying to shed the "deer in the headlights stare."

There is nothing routine about any grief journey. We can help others validate the realities of their physical maladies, emotional stressors and strains, mental depressions, sadness, guilt feelings, anger, and spiritual doubts. These realities are packed in each grief journey traveler's bags. Writing may enable survivors to expunge themselves of ailments and maladies while dumping unwanted or unneeded baggage.

Writing recalls the fondest, most precious, and intimate details of the time spent with deceased spouses. This diary of lost love furnishes a memoir of a couple's life adventure together. The story explains how they stood with and by each other through good and bad times.

Many couples enjoyed cheery times, struggled through setbacks, and survived downturns. Nothing can alter those facts or memories. Writing about the adventure, coupled with photographs, reminiscences, possessions accumulated, and personal reflections leave an indelible footprint of a life lived. Death instantly extinguished that happy life. A little piece of each widowed survivor died with their spouse. Many survivors tightly embrace those special memories. Sadly, what once was will never be again.

The cathartic impact of written memoirs and remembrances lifts personal morale, spirits, outlooks, and energies. Writing provides the strength to go on for another day, a means to share and describe the love of our lives – a love that never diminished or died.

Writings, memoirs, poems, songs, and notes may help fill some of the potholes survivors find along the path of their grief journey and keep the memories of their beloved alive. Writing provides an aperture for the survivor to talk about, share, and memorialize their past. The documentary record of "our" story may become a source of family history, a reference for future generations, a testimonial to a past life of wedded bliss, and a source of comfort for the bereaved survivor. Exercise discretion when sharing your written story to avoid overloading others.

In summary, exercise of Healing through Writing includes:

1. Documenting the story of each individual survivor, their deceased spouse, and the married life they shared.

2. The realization that death snuffed out the rest of our lives in the blink of an eye and that a piece of each survivor died with their spouse.

3. An aperture for the survivor to talk about, share, and memorialize their beloved.

4. Minimizing the risk of stressing long-term relationships to the point that they end. Remember, some folk do not know how to respond to or want to come to grips with the fact that they may ultimately face the death of their spouse.

4.11 Keeping Your Health

Kathy writes:

Just after my husband died, I lost interest in eating. I lost seven pounds in a week, and I had already been thin. As the intensity of the emotions eased, and as I found new dining partners, and learned more cooking skills, I gained the weight back over a few months. But over the next couple of years, I noticed that I was experiencing many more frequent illnesses than while my husband was alive. My body seemed to be reacting to my enormous loss.

This phenomenon seems to be very common. A number of other widows and widowers with whom I have talked about this experience have noticed similar changes in their own health. Research indicates that this phenomenon is not my imagination. As the chapter on "Changes and Getting Overwhelmed" already pointed out, the death of a spouse is ranked the most stressful event in one's life on the Holmes and Rahe Stress Scale. Stress is closely linked with health. Many widows report a sudden shift in their health status after the death of a spouse. A longitudinal study (Elwert and Christakis, 2008) suggests that the death of a spouse is a threat to the survivor's health, but the effect varies by the cause of death.

If you are a health care provider, you play an important role in helping your widowed clients to keep good health. Please be a gentle and respectful listener. Do not dismiss, judge, underestimate the loss, or give advice not based on your own experience. Listen with humility. Read Meekhof's article, entitled "5 Things a Health Care Provider Should Not Say to a Widow", on the huffingtonpost.com website, referenced under "Articles" in the "Resources" section of this book. Read the references under "Websites for Friends of Widows" in the

"Resources" section of this book. Read the chapter in this book entitled "Coping with Those Who Say or Do the Wrong Thing".

A widow told me that her late husband's physician called her on the phone a few days after he had died, to tell her what her husband should have done to take better care of his health. Those words were not helpful in saving his life. Those words did not provide comfort to the grieving widow, who was already feeling the survivor's guilt that is so common. On the other hand, there are many kind physicians who do provide words that are honest, useful, and comforting.

If you are the survivor, remember those who care about you, and those who depend on you. Take good care of yourself. Get regular checkups. Eat regular meals. Rest when you need it. Do exercise that you can enjoy. Get strength from whatever spiritual practice you have.

Don't be afraid to ask for what you need. Ask others to invite you to meals, so that you eat regularly. Join Meetup groups for dining out and for hiking, dancing, exercise, and spiritual practice. (Refer to the "Resources" section for a description of Meetup groups and how to access them.)   Leave behind those who are negative, who are judgmental about your grief, who cause stress, or who do not contribute to your spiritual growth. Or educate them, if you have the patience. Seek those people and things that give you comfort, and perhaps even joy.

John writes:

Take care of yourself! Keep after your health. Every widowed survivor must personally focus on their self-care and well-being. Each needs to be strong if they plan to move on and continue living. Others may be depending on you! Death of a spouse clouds perspective, rumples self-confidence, disrupts routine, confuses rationality, creates self-doubt, saps initiative, and may be a source of physical ailments and symptoms.

I'm still here and I am alone. There is no specified timeframe or prescribed schedule to begin or complete the course of recovery. Imperatively, each survivor necessarily must move forward, set goals, make plans, and work on a survival plan at their pace. Remember every journey begins with a first small step. Failure to move ahead means one may be stagnating or withering away. In those cases, the survivor may wish to seek counseling or treatment to jump start their healing process and sort out where they believe they are physically, mentally, emotionally, and spiritually.

The mourning period lasts as long as the survivor wants it to last. Their resolve, determination, and state of mind determine the pace they adopt on their path to recovery. The time of lamentation allows survivors to reflect, plan, and occupy their new reality.

Practice early intervention and prevention. Physically, take walks with the dog, wander into the woods, jog, exercise, date, go dancing, get out with friends, and spend time alone for prayer, reflection, and meditation, or read a book. Keep active and do not hesitate to reach out to others. There are many ways to stay physically active, but do what feels comfortable within the scope of your interests, motivations, resources, physical abilities, and energy levels. Seek treatment for medical conditions. Do not neglect your health. Obtain needed guidance, assistance, therapy, and treatment. Pay attention to rest and relaxation. Eat properly. Exercise regularly. Get enough rest and sleep.

Spiritually, pray, if that is part of your routine. Go to church, read the scripture or articles representative of your personal spiritual beliefs and values. Seek spiritual direction if you feel the need.

Some voids are filled by support groups, mentioned in Chapter 4.8: "Getting Help". Mentally, stop punishing yourself for what you think you should have done and did not do. This may be a hard step for some survivors to take because they are so guilt laden. Remember and reward yourself. Take credit for the good things you did. Keep in touch with family and friends; they will usually understand, show empathy, and be nonjudgmental. True friends and relatives will remain steadfastly loyal, no matter what. They love us for who we are and give absolute support. But realize some friends, and even family, may abandon you.

Success in maintaining personal health requires giving oneself permission to commit to self-preservation. Remember Jesus said, "Love one another as I have loved you" and "Love your neighbor as yourself".

4.12 Sorting through Possessions

Kathy writes:

My husband died suddenly and completely unexpectedly. So when I thought about giving away his things, especially in the earliest raw days, my first, irrational, thought was, "But he might need them!" I needed time just to get used to the idea that he was gone.

Dennis collected original antique clothing from the 19th and early 20th centuries, and also costumes, for his performances with the vintage dancing troupe. He acquired beautiful West African clothing for his drumming performances. Even for his everyday clothing, he selected beautiful colors and high-quality fabrics. He collected musical instruments, bicycles, camera equipment, books, and recorded music. He chose everything with care and with consideration about quality. These things, even his clothing, were so much an expression of who he was. So it has been very, very difficult for me to part with many of these things.

Holding onto Dennis's possessions for a long time felt right to me. Other widows and widowers have told me that parting with their spouses' possessions almost immediately felt right. The decision on timing is different for every widow and widower. And that is as it should be.

Many advise not to make major decisions about dispersing possessions in the first three months, because decisions made during such an emotional time may be regretted later. Some advise not to sell a house within the first year, for the same reason. Of course, the necessity to follow the instructions of a will, and to do what is necessary to survive financially, might be exceptions.

In any case, the widow/widower is the one who best knows the right time for sorting through possessions, and what should be done with them. The widow/widower is the one who knows best whether any help is needed. Here are some suggestions to survivors:

1. Don't let anyone push you! You are the one who owns the timeline. You will know when it's time. You will know from the feeling you have about it; you will feel peace instead of distress. Do not start until you are ready. Otherwise you might cause yourself unnecessary anxiety and heartache. You might make decisions you will regret later. If it is months after the death, or years, does not matter

2. Do not let anyone judge you! No one, not even another widow, knows all the considerations that go into your decisions. No one has the right to judge you.

3. Consider putting the items into storage until you are ready to go through them.

4. Take your time. Consider breaking up the work into segments an hour or two long, and then taking a break. Do a little bit at a time, and take a day off now and then. Take the pressure off yourself. Praise yourself when you accomplish something.

5. Decide whether you want help, what kind of help you want, and whom you want as your helpers. Then let your desired helpers know. If you want to limit help to moving large boxes, let your helpers know. Or if you want no help at all, let those who are inquiring know that. Some survivors feel that helpers make the process easier and provide emotional support. Others feel that helpers might make decisions about what to do with possessions that the survivor will regret later.

6. Organize the possessions into six categories, by
    moving them or labeling them:
    - Trash
    - Items to keep
    - Items to give to family member or friend
    - Donations to charitable cause
    - Items to sell
    - Items not yet decided upon

7. Start by throwing out the items labeled "Trash". That
    will quickly create more space for working with the
    other items.

8. Give away items to those who would be honored to
    receive them.

9. Determine which items are essential mementos for you
    to keep.

10. Even after you start, you might find an item that you are
    not ready to decide about. Listen to your heart, and
    wait until it feels right. Put that item into the "not yet
    decided upon" category for now.

11. Move the items not decided upon to a hidden area, and
    determine later if you missed each of those items.

12. Replace holes in your space with other possessions so
    that you will not be constantly reminded of the loss.

13. Take photographs of treasures that you must part with,
    so that you can enjoy the memories later.

14. Consider making something creative, such as a quilt,
    with fabrics from clothing that you won't use but want to
    remember.

There is no need to feel guilty about parting with possessions if you decide that you no longer need them. You are still keeping your partner's memory alive in your heart in other ways.

Expect that the process might sometimes trigger feelings of grief and loss. Allow yourself to feel those feelings, and then make your decisions. Perform the process in your own way and in your own time.

John writes:

Sorting through possessions can be onerous, fatiguing, depressing, and seemingly unending. Deciding how to deal with possessions takes thought, planning, and courage.

I decided to move back to my hometown after Nancy died. I could not fathom continuing to live in the small town where "we" were so happy; the idea was beyond my comprehension. There were too many reminders.

Within six months, I sold our house and purchased a new home. I donated her clothes to charities who could distribute them to people in need. My mother-in-law agreed with the decision to "give the clothes to where they can be used, don't let them become moth-eaten. That's the way Nancy would've wanted it." My mother-in-law's advice simplified my final decision.

With the help of friends, I held a mammoth estate sale, parted with several rooms of unneeded furniture and musical instruments, emptied the storage bin, donated thousands of books, and filled over 250 large contractor trash bags with throwaway stuff. I unloaded over 17,000 pounds of unneeded possessions! This enabled me to substantially reduce the costs of relocation. I am still getting rid of things.

Couples accumulate a lot of belongings during their marriages. I didn't care for some things we "collected" together. But if she liked something and wanted to buy the item, it was ok. We all have "connections" to souvenirs that symbolize pleasant times, happy memories, or special events. Such things are remnants of a past life with our deceased spouse. Now I can part with things I really did not care for without regret. (I needed to put myself out of the stuff's misery.) But a decision to do nothing is fine. I proceeded and chose not to look back.

The basement looked great once it was emptied and uncluttered. I had not been able to walk down there for seven years, basically since we'd moved in. Less was becoming better.

Primary targets for sale, donation, or disposal included:

1. Taking 50 containers of old documents, we toted around for 30 years, to the recycling center for incineration. The attendants and I got to know each other on a first name basis by the end of the project. Recycling saved time, money, and the ecology. I strongly recommend disposing of old files and unneeded, confidential documents through reputable recycling centers. I am still vetting old files and papers. I have learned there is no need to keep most documents for more than 5 years. But check with your legal advisor or tax specialist to determine what kind of documents to retain, for what period of time, and what you can purge.

2. We stored a host of items ranging from the belongings of deceased relatives, unused wedding presents, and unopened boxes from prior moves. We really didn't know why we were holding on to stuff. "Just because" is not a good reason to hold on to things. Initially I was

stymied by the enormity of this part of the task of purging.

Clouds of dust and mold spewed into the air as we opened old boxes and bags. The decision to immediately trash these potential health hazards was easy.

Throughout the project, I felt remorse, confusion, anger, and uncertainty. I feared the possibility of throwing something away I may want or need later. To date, I haven't really missed anything.

3, Our books, a veritable library, had to go. Many were obsolete and outdated. In our family, we were all avid readers. Nancy was an elementary school teacher/reading specialist. I was a retired adjunct professor who served on panels that previewed prepublication textbooks before final publication.

   A local second-hand book dealer took most of the books. The arrangement was a win-win. I eliminated expensive shipping costs. He bolstered his inventory. Parting with some of the books was like abandoning old friends; but it was necessary.

4. Dealing with personal belongings, sentimental items, and family treasures was difficult. I returned heirlooms to Nancy's family.   Returning this stuff to where it belonged was the right thing to do. Since my sons were both dead, I had no use for these things and my grandchildren would not understand their significance.

Family members and relatives appreciated the distributions. I sent my grandchildren things that belonged to their father, grandmother, and great grandmothers. The kids seem grateful.

Sorting through your deceased spouse's personal belongings is a labor of love that takes courage, resolve, and an emotional toll. There is no proper timetable or schedule for completing the work. Each survivor maintains final control over all decisions.

Before Nancy died, during one of our conversations we concluded possessions were only "things". When I die, they'll remain "things" and I'll have no further use for them. We enter the world with nothing and leave with nothing.

Legal considerations may dictate what to do with certain effects, possessions, and property. A last will and testament may specify an order of bequest, distribution, donation, disposition, or liquidation of belongings. (Survivors must ascertain if such instructions were left by the deceased.)

I have heard of cases where survivors have not changed anything in the spaces where their spouses "lived". They report leaving the space just as it was the last time their beloved was there. In essence, the space becomes a shrine. Some simply close the door to the space and periodically dust or clean, leaving the contents otherwise undisturbed.

Grant yourself permission to sort through and dispose of unneeded possessions. Consider that some of these things may be useful to others. Cleaning out is OK. Purging can be a sign one is on the road to recovery and moving with life. But choosing to do nothing is perfectly acceptable.

4.13 Prolonged Grief

Kathy writes:

Some diagnosticians use the term "complicated grief" to refer to grief that lasts so long and is so intense that it is incapacitating. This term, "complicated grief", can be confusing, because it sounds too much like the conditions described in our chapter that we called "Nonstandard Circumstances of Grief". So we chose to use the term "prolonged grief", because it refers less ambiguously to the intensity of grief lasting longer than usual in a way that disrupts the grieving person's life.

Is there really such a thing as prolonged grief? After the death of a loved one, normal feelings include intense emotions, shock, fear, guilt, loss, sadness, anger, yearning for the loved one, inability to concentrate, and sleep disturbances. And we know that each person grieves in their own way and in their own time. There is no universal timetable for grief. So can we really say how long grief should last? Can we judge that, if someone grieves longer than some standard time, that this person is experiencing prolonged grief, and must undergo some kind of treatment?

These are difficult questions to answer with black-and-white certainty. I think the real answer is to ask yourself what you, the one doing the grieving, feel. Is your grieving interfering with your ability to interact with other people, to work, to take care of yourself and any who depend on you, and to seek happiness? Have the sensations of grieving become unbearable? Have you given yourself time (at least several months, perhaps longer) to work through the initial raw sensations of grief?

The popular idea that one will "get over" grief, or "move on", is a misconception. Those who have suffered a loss do not simply return to their original emotional state before the loss. Instead, they learn to adapt to the loss, and they integrate the life of the loved one, and the loss, into their memories, and into their own continued personal growth. A study by Carnelley, Wortman, Bolger, and Burke (2006) suggests that it is normal for those who have lost a spouse to experience memories and engage in conversations about their late spouse for decades after the loss. One time I had to explain to someone that I do not just forget someone I knew for forty years. I will not pretend that someone so much a part of my life did not exist. I still feel some emotions about him. That does not mean that I have prolonged grief.

Six years has passed, at this writing, since Dennis died, and I have noticed that the intensity of the raw emotions that I felt just after his death has decreased. I still love him, wish he were alive with me, and still experience an occasional "grief attack". But I am able to concentrate on writing, to interact with other people, and even to enjoy attending someone's wedding.

If someone else tells you that you have prolonged grief, do not just accept it. Instead, use their observation as an opportunity to ask yourself some questions. Perhaps it is their own lack of understanding of grief that led to their observation. On the other hand, ask yourself the questions listed above, and listen to your own answers. Is your grief interfering with your life, and have you given yourself enough time? Do you just need more time? Have you noticed any changes, any lessening of the intensity?

If you do feel that you are experiencing prolonged grief that interferes with your normal functioning, then I recommend you seek out a good therapist who knows about grief. Ask other widows and widowers for advice on who might be a good therapist or counselor. Or ask the coordinator of a grief support group, or hospice. I recommend finding someone who does therapy involving talking sessions, not someone who will just write a prescription, although prescriptions can sometimes be beneficial. I like to work with someone who has a Ph.D. in psychology, but that is my experience. There are good therapists with master's degrees, and good counselors affiliated with churches, especially if they have experience working with those who are grieving. A referral from someone has worked with the practitioner can be very helpful.

Refer to the "Resources" section in the back of this book for other sources of help. Call the National Suicide Prevention Lifeline (1-800-273-TALK (8255)) if you feel desperate enough to be considering suicide, or if you just need someone to talk to.

John writes:

Prolonged grief, which most often occurs after the death of a spouse, can be described as being mired down in grief. People who have been stuck in a grief mode for long, extended periods may be suffering from prolonged or chronic grief. I have read that clinical evidence supports the concept of prolonged grief as a disease but not the clinical diagnosis. Prolonged or complicated grief differs from "Nonstandard Circumstances of Grief", discussed in Chapter 4.5.

Prolonged grief can be caused by situations and circumstances that bombard the survivor after the death of a spouse. Symptoms of prolonged grief may cause survivors to isolate or withdraw. Some survivors become so debilitated by the loss of their spouse they have difficulty coping with their new reality. Some of the fallout is temporary and some may become permanent.

Death of a spouse casts one's life situation onto a collision course, which adds to existing turmoil, disruption, and confusion. Living day-to-day life is already a state of dishevelment, disruption, flux, and transition. One will generally recognize their new life situation. Hence they choose to embrace or resist the reality of change. Prolonged grief means one may be suffering with feelings of hopelessness and abandonment.

Dr. Bonnie J. Miller, MSN, D. Min, nationally known nursing consultant, speaker, author, and Professor Emeritus of Nursing at Xavier University in Cincinnati, shares a bright outlook about overcoming prolonged grief. Dr. Miller suggests a survivor may say, "Now each significant event, Christmas, birthdays, holidays, anniversaries of wonderful trips taken, etc. generate conversations with the deceased from giving thanks for the past to, in my case, reminding the deceased that had he been here the celebration would be beautiful and the gift wrapped more beautifully. Prolonged grief does not have to be heavy and sad. Sometimes it can bring laughter and joy."

The main assertion herein is that overwhelming grief, incredible shock, waiting for information, finishing business, and following external rules can contribute to prolonged grief. Nothing may be resolved until we find answers, receive clinical help, and develop skills to cope with the reality of the situation. Each roadblock, setback, or delay in moving toward closure creates prolonged grief. There is no moving forward until the survivor decides to do so.

4.14 Bitter or Better

Kathy writes:

A question that survivors face is this: Am I bitter or better? Has the tragedy in my life overcome me, so that I see only loss? Or am I somehow able to incorporate the loss into my own personal growth, and perhaps into new ways to express myself creatively, or to help others?

I was inspired by the book *Radical Survivor* by Nancy Saltzman (refer to the "Resources" section at the end of this book for the complete reference). Nancy was a breast cancer survivor before she lost her husband and both her sons in a plane crash. Nancy started an organization she called "Breast Friends" to help newly diagnosed women with breast cancer to understand what they would experience and to receive support from other survivors. After the crash, Nancy returned to her position as school principal and helped the children of the school, who knew her sons, to work through their own grief. With the school staff and students, she found many ways to memorialize her family. She also connected with other survivors of similar tragedies. She was devastated by the tragedy, but found ways to make positive change based on her experience.

Not all of us can do what Nancy did, but we might be able to do smaller, less public things that could help ourselves and other people. Loss gives us a glimpse into the essence of life that others without loss might not see. Sometimes we can help them to see. I know someone who has lost his whole family, and who observes others around him. When he sees someone, even a stranger, not honoring his own family members, sometimes he will say something to remind that person that the fragile nature of life urges us to honor those we love, or should love. His own tragedy gives him credibility and strength. I greatly admire his actions to reach out.

Loss also helps us to empathize with others going through loss. Joining a grief support group helps us to receive support, and also to give support. Giving to others, especially without expectation of getting anything back, can help us to find meaning. When we do not expect anything back, then we are not disappointed if we get nothing back, and we are pleasantly surprised if we do get something back.

Finding a way to memorialize our loved ones helps us to know that others will remember also. Memorializing is a way to create some immortality, in a sense, for those we love. Making a donation, setting a marker in a public place, planting a memorial tree, writing a memoir, posting on a memorial website, or setting up a memorial scholarship are some examples.

Sometimes we go back and forth between bitter and better. We might need to go through the "bitter" part to release feelings of sorrow, anger, or a sense of unfairness. Then during the "better" phase, we reach out to others, or create new things, or find peace in our spiritual practice. In a way, both of these phases, if we use them well, are necessary to our further growth. The bitter phase is a time of releasing, of emptying. We cannot just bottle up these feelings. They are real, and must be expressed. Sometimes we must separate ourselves from others who do not understand, during this time, so that we do not hurt them or ourselves. Sometimes we can spend this time, or part of it, with others who understand. We should acknowledge to ourselves that we are using this time for releasing, and that this phase does perform a valuable function that we need.

John writes:

Nancy and I met Brad and Emily through a grief support group
for bereaved parents. Their grief journey began years ago
when their beloved adult child perished in a vehicular
accident. They still mourn the death.

Brad and Emily shared their belief that every grief survivor's
journey begins with two questions; **"Do I want to live or die?"**
and **"Do I want to be bitter or better?"** These seemingly
simple questions are very complex and cut to the core of
every widowed survivor's dilemma, especially those whose
grief is more recent.

One can easily be bitter one day and better the next. One's
moods remain variable, volatile, and unpredictable, depending
upon the day and the circumstances in play at the time. Life
may settle down for a while; then some untoward stimulus can
topple the apple cart. Such may be a random, happenstance
situation or event that triggers a memory or emotion of a sad
or happy time. No one can predict what could stir things to
cause a shift from bitter to better or better to bitter. When the
change occurs, a secondary ripple effect comes into play,
forcing the widowed survivor to contemplate whether they
want to live or die in that particular moment.

If a stimulus evokes a happy memory, a survivor may want to
dwell in the moment; remain in a favorable, positive frame of
mind; and continue to recall the pleasant reminiscences.
However, if the trigger invokes painful, unhappy, sad
recollections, the survivor may wilt, retreat, and want to die in
the moment to forget.

During a grief journey, the traveler frequently vacillates
between bitter or better, striving to maintain a delicate
balance. Mood swings, spiritual doubts, physical ailments,
chronic depression, and emotional distress are common.
Each survivor makes choices appropriate to their current life

situation. As mentioned previously, each unique grief journey consists of a complex combination of multiple variables, and no two people have exactly the same type of experience.

Hopefully, as survivors continue walking the grief journey path, they experience more "better" days than "bitter" ones. The journey takes time and cannot be rushed.

Some widowed survivors become hopelessly convinced they will never recover from the death of their spouse. But others hone their coping skills and do come to grips with their loss. They project serenity, acceptance, and calmness. Does one ever totally recover from the loss of their soul mate, life companion, lover, best friend, or partner? Many survivors proclaim pain subsides with the passage of time, but report they'll never forget their beloved.

Choosing to be bitter or better can account for the ways family, friends, and others may respond to the survivor. Family and friends, based on their observations of the survivor's demeanor, decide how they may approach future relationships and contacts. At times survivors emit confusing signals. Confusion is a normal response and assessment for those who may not have experienced sadness, death, or grief.

Part 5. Creating a New Life

Part 5 focuses on the creation of a new life, as the survivor recovers from the initial shock and finds new ways to cope with the loss. These chapters describe the process of making new decisions without the partner, giving yourself permission to change, strategies for developing new relationships, where to live, traveling, financial survival, work, and finding a new identity.

Creating a new life inherently means a survivor has committed to moving ahead, despite the loss of their spouse, into their new, unknown future with confidence, vision, and hope.

5.1 Making Decisions without Your Partner

Kathy writes:

You probably became used to making major decisions, and even some minor decisions, with your partner, especially if you were married for a long time. Now all that is gone. Now even relatively minor decisions – at what restaurant to dine, how to spend the day, where to go on vacation, whom to hire to cut the grass – must be made alone. Even more difficult are major decisions – how to invest money, when to retire, where to live, how to take care of yourself in old age – also must be made alone. At least it might seem that way in the beginning. The alternative is to enlist someone else – an offspring, a sibling, a niece or nephew, a close friend, or a professional – to participate in major decisions. In any case, there is a major adjustment to be made.

Some people come to enjoy the freedom of making decisions on their own. For some who were in relationships in which the other person tended to make most of the decisions, the freedom now to make decisions might seem a refreshing change. Others appreciate feedback and advice that might help them to make better decisions.

As we age, we might become less able to make decisions independently. Consider choosing the right people now, before reaching extreme old age, to help make decisions if you become unable to make them. A discussion with close friends and family members might be a good idea. After that discussion, an attorney can help draw up the appropriate documents.

If you have children, you might find that they volunteer to participate in decision-making. Sometimes children might be sensitive to allow you to do as much as you can, and as much as you want to do, by yourself, before stepping in to help, in a participative manner. Other times, children might barge into decision-making without your consent and participation. In either case, you will need to communicate your preferences in order to get your needs met.

If you do not have children, it might be more difficult to choose someone that you can trust to help participate in decision-making. If you choose a relative, you might want to choose one whose values are close to yours, with good communication skills. If you choose a friend, it should be a close friend, certainly one that you trust, and a friendship that is likely to last. Perhaps the relative or friend should be someone younger, in case you need decisions made if you become incapacitated in older age. If you choose a professional, it should be someone whose compensation is not tied to the decision that you make. Financial advisors that are "fee-only" do not receive commissions based on the investment you choose, so their advice is more likely to be more objective. You are vulnerable to those who might take advantage of you, and you need to be very careful with these choices.

John writes:

Naturally, most widowed survivors and their spouses spent a lot of time together during their married life. They jointly collaborated, coordinated, communicated, and cooperated on matters that affected them and their family. They planned social calendars, shopping trips, recreational activities, routine appointments, family gatherings, vacations, time to hang out together, and time away from each other. Their lives were in sync. The idiosyncratic systems, methods, and protocol for coordinating a joint life together may have seemed weird to others, but served as a comfortable and workable routine for them. Their married existence was a well-oiled mechanism without need for tinkering, adjustment, recalibration, or maintenance. They understood and knew the rules, procedures, and the expectations; no one else needed to do so.

Generally, one never made a major decision independently of the other. Exceptions possibly included surprise celebrations, special events, reaching significant milestones, or attaining some long-term ambitions or dreams.

Death of a spouse is a game changer for which no one is ever prepared. Many survivors did not immediately comprehend the scope of what the death of their spouse really meant or the related impact. An immediate reality becomes standing alone without any backup. A spouse's death represents an unprecedented adjustment in the survivor's life. To survive one must make decisions without the counsel of their partner. Of course, this comment does not discount or imply that family members, close friends, and others are unavailable for consultation and guidance. The initial ante, adapting to a widowed life status, is a tough, hard, cold fact. Many survivors may naturally approach the reality of their new "aloneness" with uncertainty, trepidation, and self-doubt.

Some survivors compare the initial stages of their widowhood to being "orphaned". The assertion lends credence to the fact that the bereaved is alone again, perhaps for the first time since they met their beloved during the days of their courtship. The intimacy, security, and companionship provided through married life are gone!

Many will find peace and relief by clinging to the memories of the good old days. Comfort resonates in "what used to be". And while the past may be a source of temporary tranquility, it does not serve the need for continuing on in the present reality. Survivors need to affirmatively take the initiative, exercise the flexibility, and do what needs to be done. Sadly, some are so stunned they do not know where to turn, what to do, or how to do it. Others realize and understand that poor choices or bad decisions can negatively impact the rest of their life, so they become carefully scrupulous.

In the cases of domestically violent, volatile, and contentious relationships, the survivor's emotions, sentiments, and reflections may be totally different. Lack of harmony in a marriage creates a dysfunctional aura with sad memories, disrupted emotions, and apathetic attitudes. Survivors of this kind of a relationship may mourn differently, if at all.

No matter what the nature of the marital relationship, in the wake of the death of a spouse the survivor still stands alone. Starting a new life means new beginnings. Solitude and independence, the survivor's new partners, encouragingly say, **"Stand on your own two feet."**

5.2 Honoring Wishes

Kathy writes:

Sometimes there is conflict between the urge to honor the wishes of the person who died versus giving yourself permission to change. Both have validity.

Dennis dearly loved his cat, and I know he would have wanted me to take very good care of him. I intend to honor that wish. I see owning a pet as a lifelong commitment. I know there are things in his life that he would not want revealed, because he did not reveal them. I intend to honor his wish for privacy. He loved to hear me play the harp, and I know he would have wanted me to continue playing. I know that the reason why he wanted to hear me play was partly that he knew that I loved making music, and he wanted me to fulfill those creative needs. I intend to honor those wishes, because I have the same wishes.

Dennis really enjoyed his own musical instruments. Selling his instruments will be difficult for me, but I do intend to sell them. Would he have wanted me to sell them after his death? I don't really know, but I think he would have been fine with it, given that he is no longer here to play them. Dennis wanted to live at the ocean, but I do not plan to move there now. Would Dennis have wanted me to move to the ocean after his death? I think he would have wanted me to do only what made me happy.

In fact, I can't think of anything that Dennis might have wanted me to do after his death that I don't want to do. We didn't talk about it, since he died so suddenly and unexpectedly. I think only that he would have wanted me to have joy in my life. He was someone always ready to experience joy, and he radiated that to others.

I heard about a widow who had very different taste in interior decorating from her husband, but she accommodated his taste while he was alive. When he died, she redecorated to her own taste. That seems reasonable to me. She is the one who has to continue to live in her house. Redecorating to her own taste does not seem like an act that dishonors her late husband.

On the other hand, if a commitment was made to the one who died, and the wish is reasonable, and is something that will not cause harm, it should be carried out. Wishes should not be ignored if to do so would dishonor the dead person. Wishes that have to do with the disposition of the deceased person's body should be carried out, unless there is some mitigating circumstance that makes the wish difficult to perform.

Those wishes that affect only the *living* need not be carried out if they are not also the wishes of the survivor. Sometimes those who have died have instructed survivors not to have a memorial service. But the memorial service is really for the benefit of those who survive. So I think that the survivors who need a memorial service should have one, regardless of any instructions.

Even when there are wishes that seem unnecessary to carry out, the survivor might feel guilty about violating their deceased partner's instructions. To proceed will require giving yourself permission to do something different, or to grow and change. Sometimes it helps to ask yourself the question what the person who died would want for you now. Sometime asking that question is not enough. Discussing the situation with a therapist who understands the grieving process might help.

John writes:

Most widowed survivors would prefer to avoid the dilemma of making decisions alone. Some situations can be intimidating and daunting (See Chapter 5.1: "Making Decisions without Your Partner".) Granting yourself permission becomes a key step to moving ahead without guilt, remorse, or second-guessing.

Precious memories of the past times remain relished treasures. Our beloved is no longer a viable resource, consultant, or second opinion for anticipated decisions or changes. Some survivors find that reminiscences of past conversations with their spouse can become beneficial in certain situations. Historical reflection, when questioning what the deceased spouse might have done, can provide useful reference points for the survivor to consider. I characterize this process as "voices from the grave".

Finding one's own pathway, after the spouse's death, can be challenging. Walking into a new life can seem uncomfortable, awkward, and scary. Nothing can change or replace the conveniences of the good old days.

Do not confuse solitude and independence. In widowhood, a survivor stands alone (**solitude**). The reality of carrying on means becoming accustomed to functioning without counsel, sanction, or permission (**independence**). Widowhood may mean solitude. But solitude does not negate the independence an individual needs for making choices or decisions. Independence means not having to be accountable to anyone else, being able to act alone without obtaining prior approval, and having the ability and the means to stand on your own. Living the new life translates into exercising independence and beginning anew.

Solitude means being alone, possibly living a solitary life, but not necessarily becoming a hermit. Independence may include being alone, but it does not require solitude. Independence does not exclude reaching out to others for help, guidance, and assistance. However, independence does mean one exercises final control over many matters.

Independence may signal the survivor's willingness to embrace a new reality and a new life. Their new **NOW** awaits discovery and exploration. This realization can be uplifting, mood changing, and positive. In the final rendering, wanting to honor the wishes of our beloved departed is indeed heroic, noble, and sweet. Thus the survivor's new reality may mean making the decision to move ahead.

Dr. Shirley reminds me, God specifically commits to always being with us. God never gives up on us and never fails. God's Spirit brings things to our remembrance as we need them. God was with us in the past, during good times and bad. God is with us today and wants the best for us. God is with us tomorrow, whatever or wherever the adventure will be.

5.3 New Relationships

Kathy writes:

The loss of a partner is a profound shift not only for the survivor, but also for all the relationships that the survivor shares with other people. When the survivor experiences such a shattering event as the loss of a loved one, it is inevitable that relationships that the survivor shares with other people will be affected. Old relationships may change or be lost, and new relationships may be formed. This chapter discusses issues that the survivor faces with friendships, the potential for new love relationships, the question of timing, strategies for developing new relationships, and Internet dating.

Friendships

One of the great lessons I learned when Dennis died was the importance of a community of friends. I think it would have provided so much more comfort and support if I had already been part of a larger community of friends when he died. This might be especially important for those widows who are childless. Dennis and I were best friends as well as spouses, and shared nearly all the same interests. We worked together, played music together, danced together, hiked together, and more. Because we were childless, he was my whole family. So when he died, my whole family died. We had common friends, but we rarely did things with other friends without each other. After he died, I suddenly needed real friends for companionship. The community was much more important than I had ever thought.

We had friends who were couples, but it was difficult and uncomfortable to maintain some of these relationships after Dennis's death. These friendships mostly faded away. The loss of these friendships after widowhood can be very painful. The loss of the spouse increases vulnerability to the pain from the loss of friendships.

So I find myself working on the task of trying to create new friendships. Grief support groups are a good resource for possible friends. These groups tend to be very accepting and friendly, and the other members understand the difficulties that other widows are experiencing. But most widows have children, and many have jobs, and those things compete for the time of these potential new friends. Often the group meets for special events, but there may be little or no contact outside the group events, especially in the beginning stages of contact.

Meetup groups are another good source for potential friends (refer to the "Resources" section). Each group focuses on a specific interest such as hiking, photography, playing music, travel, and so forth. Or the group might share characteristics such as widowhood, or belonging to a particular age group. As a result, each member of the group shares an interest in common with the other members, which tends to facilitate conversation. Again, there may be little contact outside the group events, and the other participants might be very busy. Making new friends, real friends as opposed to acquaintances, is a process that can take a great deal of time.

There are many other venues where one can meet new friends, such as volunteer organizations, places of work, religious congregations, dances, exercise groups, and organizations that focus on particular interests or hobbies. These venues are just examples of the many possible sources for new friendships.

Developing good friendships is particularly important for those widows and widowers who might not wish to get involved in a new love relationship. Those friendships will become part of the support system that can help ease the loneliness after the loss of a partner. But that support system is important for everyone, even those who do become involved in a new love relationship. That is the lesson I learned.

Love Relationships

Some widows and widowers decide that they do not wish to seek another love interest or partner after the loss of their loved one. Interestingly, there are studies (Davidson 2001, 2002) that contradict the stereotype that the depth of grief is the reason why some widows do not seek another partner. Instead, the research suggests that women who do not seek new partners are most often motivated by their new freedom, and the desire not to have to take care of another person again. Men who have not found a new partner tend to be motivated by concerns about their older age, their health, and their desirability as a partner. But the studies suggest that widowers do tend to be more ready than widows to get involved in a new relationship. More widows explicitly decide not to seek another partner.

Whether or not to seek another partner is an individual decision, and both choices are valid. We should not let anyone push us into a decision in either direction. We should not let someone else decide for us that it is too soon, or not soon enough. The best decision is to make your own decision and to take the time you need in making it.

Can I ever love again? Do I want to? Am I loveable?

The feelings of longing for the lost partner might be so intense, especially in the beginning, that the survivor might feel that she or he can never fall in love again with anyone else.

Some survivors find themselves alone after many decades in a marriage or committed relationship. If they decide to seek a new relationship now, it might feel as if they had stepped out of a time machine. The rules might all have changed. Now there are different dating rules of etiquette, and even different health considerations than there were 30 or 40 years ago. Now there is texting, and Internet dating websites (more on this topic in a later section). A woman picking up some or all of the tab is considered more acceptable. Often people meet at the date site, rather than the man picking up the woman first. Sexually transmitted diseases are more deadly than in the 60s and 70s. These are just a few examples.

For some, their lost partner was their first love. They never experienced partnering with a different person with different likes and dislikes, a different personality, and different physical characteristics. For these people, it might seem overwhelming to date someone new.

Then there is the question of one's own desirability. We have all grown older, and our habits have hardened over time. We might have become less flexible and open than in our youth. We might have lost muscle tone, and gained weight, wrinkles, and gray hair. Our health might not be as pristine. Our time here has grown shorter. We might begin to question our ability to partner with someone new, or the possibility that anyone would want to partner with us.

But others have also grown older. They have the same trepidations that we have. There are many others in the same situation. There are many who are looking for someone real, not perfect.

How Soon

In my first grief support group, two of us had new losses, only a month or two old. We asked the two group facilitators, "How long should we wait before dating?" They both said "Two years." The two of us with new losses looked at each other in dismay. Neither of us could imagine tolerating this complete isolation for two years.

In retrospect, maybe the facilitators were right. After a great loss, there is a condition called "on the rebound", characterized by strong emotions, neediness, and longing for the lost partner that is too easily transferred into longing for the first person one meets. During this "rebound" period, it is too easy to make poor decisions about new relationships, or to make new commitments too soon. It's better to wait, if possible, until these emotions become calmer.

For some, this might take two years, or longer. For others, maybe it can take a few months. I have heard of cases in which someone happily married lost their spouse, then remarried only a few months later, and stayed married. Sometimes relationships that begin so early in the grieving process can turn out to be lasting.

But it is still a good idea to proceed with caution when one is still feeling so emotional. Again, this is an individual decision. No one else but the grieving survivor can make this decision. But it might be a good idea to talk to a counselor or therapist to help get perspective and advice on when to begin, and to help you to ask yourself the right questions, and to answer them honestly.

Strategies for Developing New Relationships

In that first grief support group, the group facilitators warned us about divorced people. "They're bitter," they said. Divorce can also be a very traumatic experience of great loss, and those who have suffered it deserve our compassion. But it is different from the death of a spouse. Divorced people often have negative feelings for their former partner. They might be more eager to go on to a new relationship and forget the old one. In contrast, widowed people often still feel much love for their lost partner. We did not seek out or negotiate the end of our relationship. The end was not our choice. Those who are divorced might not understand our continued love for the one we lost. They might even feel jealousy. Some might demand that we take down photographs and reminders of our lost one, might push us to dispose of possessions before we are ready, and might resent our expressions of grief.

Other widowed people are more likely to understand our grief and our continued feelings of love for our lost partner, because they themselves share those experiences. In a relationship with someone also widowed, you might find yourselves talking about your lost partners, remembering special anniversaries, and sharing experiences of grief. In many ways, a relationship with someone widowed can be easier because of that shared understanding.

But there are many other factors to consider in determining compatibility, and those who are widowed often can form good lasting relationships with those who are not widowed, especially if they are very empathetic and compassionate people.

Grief support groups are good places to meet those who might be compatible. But do not approach those groups with expectations of meeting a partner. Their purpose is to provide support to others who are grieving, and to receive grief support, not to seek a partner. Instead, allow any resulting relationship to evolve naturally, or not. Meetup groups with those who share your interests are good places to meet new friends (refer to the "Resources" section), and some friendships might evolve into love relationships. Again, it is best to approach these groups without expectations.

On the other hand, Internet dating websites have been designed specifically for meeting people who might become love interests. Sometimes it is a faster way to find others who are compatible and who are also seeking a love interest. There are pros and cons to Internet dating, and precautions that should be taken, which will be discussed in the next section.

Internet Dating and Safety Tips

Using an Internet dating website, or even multiple websites, can be a way to quickly find and meet people who are also interested in meeting someone and who might be compatible with you. You can choose a generic dating website, or a dating website for those who have special interests such as a religious, spiritual, or political affiliation or lifestyle choice. Sometimes a special-interest website can help narrow down your search for someone, to ensure that you meet people with common interests and values.

The website will allow you to define your "profile", which will specify your characteristics, and what characteristics you seek in someone else. Characteristics can include age, physical characteristics, marital status, geographic location, religious or spiritual affiliations, political preferences, dietary preferences, whether you smoke or drink, and what type of relationship you seek, for example. The website allows you and the other members to search for compatible profiles. You have the option to send messages through the website to others, or to respond to messages from others. The process is anonymous, because everyone uses a nickname of their choosing. But the website usually encourages members to provide a photograph.

The next step is to get involved in corresponding with one or more other members of the website. You might find that there is someone who intrigues you more than the others. Take your time corresponding before going to the next step, to get a good idea what the person is like. At this point, it is best not to give out identifying information, such as your complete name, your address, or your phone number. Remain completely anonymous until you are sure about this person.

The person that you are corresponding with could be anyone, not what they present in messages. I know of a case in which a woman thought she was falling in love with a man, but it turned out to be a woman! People could represent themselves falsely as being from a different country, with different interests, or anything at all. But the website probably has a facility for reporting such people and blocking them. Most people are sincere and genuine. Be cautious, but also realize that communicating is very safe until you identify who you are. So it makes sense to correspond as if people are genuine, but keep in mind that you do not really know them yet.

During the correspondence stage, you might be tempted to form fantasies about who this person is, and even to get emotionally involved. Again, try to keep in mind that you do not really know this person yet. No matter how much you have corresponded, you will not really know them until you meet them in person. For that reason, if you are truly interested, it is a good idea not to correspond too long before talking on the phone and meeting. Correspond long enough to feel safe, but not so long that you build up unrealistic fantasies.

The next step is to talk on the phone. Do this before actually meeting, to rule out anyone whom you would not want to meet. If you wish to remain anonymous and safe, do not give out your own phone number. Take the other's phone number, block caller ID on your phone, and then make the call. Talk openly, but don't give out your phone number, address, or last name.

After corresponding for a time, and talking on the phone several times, the next step is to meet in person. If you wish to be extra cautious, you can perform an online background check, including criminal check, for a fee, before meeting for the first time.

Meet in a public place, where you can easily get help if you need it, and where you can get away safely. Let a friend or family member know where you are going and when you expect to return.

If the person passes your tests, gradually you can choose to give out your phone number, your full name, and other identifying information, and eventually invite the person to your residence. Even at this point, be careful not to make any commitments too soon, or allow the person to move into your house until you are truly ready. Remember the "rebound" phenomenon, discussed earlier in this chapter. Taking precautions in the beginning is easier than extricating yourself later.

In the book *Epilogue* (2008), the author Anne Roiphe describes her dating experiences, many of them using online websites, after the death of her husband. Like many others, she has both good and bad experiences. Sometimes it is possible to make good lasting friendships from these websites even when they do not deliver romantic relationships. I have one good friend I still talk with often on the phone, and one or two others that I correspond with on occasion. I know at least one widower who met his wife, a widow, on a dating website, and they are still happily married. I know of others who used dating websites but have not ended up with a lasting romantic relationship. Experiences with these websites vary. Some like them; others do not. They are not a panacea, but they are just one of many ways to meet people.

John writes:

"My spouse died! I'm alone! What now?" This not so uncommon quandary vexes many survivors, especially the newly widowed. "Should I seek new friends and new relationships?" In the context of this chapter, new relationships are not necessarily limited to dating. New relationships or friendships can develop through support groups, affiliations with new organizations, or with folks in special interest groups or activities the survivor may join.

New relationships materialize in unusual circumstances, strange forms, odd shapes, and perplexing subtleties. Social circles, from the past, included family and friends. Social circles will continue to include the former friends, but may also expand to include new acquaintances. Situations can become uneasy and tense if the survivor is the only widowed member of their former social groups. However, do not abandon your existing friends and social contacts.

In support groups, connections are forged through contacts, unwritten understandings, and unspecified traditions. These groups believe and accept "it's ok to be wherever you are."

Relationships begin in many types of settings including, but not limited to, participation in therapy groups, support groups, church groups, and other meetings dedicated to helping widowed survivors. Such groups may have multiple venues for support, social, educational, and therapeutic opportunities and purposes. Some groups are sponsored by national, state, and local organizations, churches, hospitals, hospices, funeral homes, social service agencies, or widowed survivors simply reaching out to each other.

The act of reaching out has helped many widowed survivors gain a sense of healing. The quasi-therapeutic, educational, social, and support groups are vital, inexpensive, user friendly channels which help begin the convalescence from the pangs of grief and bereavement.

Widowed survivors tend to be more sensitive to each other. The timing is rife for forging new friendships and relationships with other bereaved survivors and support groups.

A survivor realizes "we" were a couple once, and so does every member of the "old" group. (The "I" and "we" dilemma was discussed in Chapter 4.3: "Challenges and Getting Overwhelmed".) Survivors rationalize "You" are still a couple. Now "I" am alone! The widowed survivor may feel out of place, insecure, alone, and misunderstood. Some of the following ideas, notions, or thoughts seem pertinent. Survivors may naturally ask themselves:

- Am I just an add-on?
- Do I still fit within this group of people?
- Did they invite me because they feel sorry for me?
- They all have each other and I have no one. I don't know where I need to be. Do they really want me around? Where do I belong?
- I'm uncomfortable and feel out of place.
- No one understands where I am, how I feel, or what I'm going through.
- I hate being alone.
- Life will never be as it was.

Some survivors have reported that their relationships and friendships with other married couples dissolved after they became widowed. Why? Because intact couples, those who have not lost a spouse, also ask some of the same questions or silently share the uneasiness mentioned above. Without asking, married group members question, "Why are you here?" Many survivors reported that their "former" circle of friends continued to function, but intentionally excluded them, the widowed survivor. While excluding the widowed survivor may seem hurtful, simply some circles are "married only"; widowed folk do not fit.

Reasons given for excluding survivors are:

"We're all married; you're alone. We think you don't belong here anymore." One may feel shunned and ostracized, as a social misfit. The presumed insinuation hurts. But the rude, heartless, cold, unspoken reality is "we don't really feel comfortable having you around. Go away and be with other widowed people like you."

Survivors query, "Who do these people think they are? Why are they so bigoted, narrow-minded, hard-nosed, and mean-spirited?" Their conduct is based on fear that the survivor's misfortune may strike them…and one day it will. They do not know what to say to the survivor, even though the survivor has not changed. It's just the former "us" is now a "me". And, previously the former "us" was part of the group. The group only has room for two of "us", not a single "me".

A widowed survivor disrupts the balance and flow of the group. Sometimes people feel uneasy about moving beyond their comfort zones. They may even believe the widowed survivor is different, and possibly a threat. The widowed survivor's presence makes the scene guarded, tense, and awkward.

Friends do not care about what happened or how it used to be. They abide by their unposted sign, **"for couples only"**. Widowed survivors might as well be aliens. Groups shun any reminder that the death of a spouse is a tragedy that may befall them at any time.

There are no set rules, formulae, templates, or taboos for forming new relationships. Humans are social beings by nature. So in the aftermath of the death of a spouse, during the early stages of mourning, the newly widowed may more easily identify with other survivors.

Friendships

The challenges cited earlier may provide the incentive for growing new friendships. New relationships seem to begin quickly, especially among recently bereaved survivors. Connections are generally devoid of the traps, expectations, prejudgments, and pitfalls that may befall relationships with others who have not lost a spouse. One may be more at ease by socializing with others who are already walking the path of a grief journey. Widowed survivors readily understand other widowed survivors. Such an abundance of resources and experience may also help a new survivor avert becoming a victim to predatory scams.

Formalities of the new friendship formation dynamic are abridged because other widowed survivors understand the pain and know the landscape. Senior survivors understand where a new survivor has been, what he or she has suffered, and, generally how one might be feeling. Experience serves as both a great teacher and a cruel master.

In these protective settings, a widowed survivor can freely express emotion and still be accepted without fear of judgment, ridicule, or reprisal. Newly widowed survivors may feel safer, less vulnerable, more relaxed, and readily accepted.

Can I Ever Love Again? Do I Want To? Am I Loveable?

Many survivors admit to asking these questions. They have expressed similar concerns. Each survivor's grief journey, experience, feelings, and mindset is different. Basic answers are yes, no, never, maybe, I don't know, why, not now, who cares, or basically anything is possible. Potential responses reveal a universe of possibilities and scenarios.

Some bereaved feel they are betraying their beloved for entertaining the notion of ever loving again. This mindset can be difficult to change. Our deceased mate will always hold a special piece of our heart. We will love them forever. Many believe their deceased beloved would want them to be happy again and move on with life.

Some of the variations in the responses backtrack to the question of what was the quality of the married relationship. Was the time spent together enjoyable and mutually supportive? Was the marriage mutually satisfactory and passionate? Was the relationship dysfunctional, stormy, and on the rocks, prone to domestic violence and spousal abuse? Were the parties to the marriage happy or did they just go through the motions? Were partners sensitive to each other? Did they love, care for, and respect each other? Were they mean, antagonistic, malicious, and apathetic toward each other? Answers influence how the widowed survivor may feel about the three questions in the title of this subchapter.

If a widowed survivor should ever encounter another love, many know the intensity of past passions and amity may never be replicated. Remaining open-minded to new possibilities is healthy. If the survivor chooses to love again, many understand they can still have the capacity to love another person. How many widowed survivors have remarried?

"Do I want to remarry?" is another question. Some survivors have no desire to remarry, become involved with another, or even have new friends of the opposite gender. They may proclaim, "I had the best and that best can never be replaced." Some widowed survivors believe they can never again experience the love, intimacy, closeness, or depth of a caring relationship with another. Some make new friends and develop new hobbies, interests, activities, and social calendars. Each individual's right to choose is sacrosanct.

- Am I loveable? Good question!
- Do I want to be loved? Can I let myself be? Will I give myself permission to be? What holds me back?
- Do I want to belong and want to be part of something and someone else?
- Do I want to be remarried or just have some close and good friends?
- Why do I project a stiff-necked, tough, rigid, fearless image?

Chameleon manifestations of stubbornness, false pride, toughness, no nonsense independence, and projecting "I don't need anyone" may hold many back. This posturing portrays the exact opposite of what survivors are really seeking, namely being with other people. Psychologists might diagnose these shenanigans as antisocial behavior, oppositional defiance, anxiety neurosis, or chronic depression.

Some believe that having many friends with whom they can socialize is fine. Such helps lessen solitude, isolation, and loneliness. I prefer to believe these actions signify the survivor is remaining open to all possibilities and options.

How soon?

Good question! No standard answers. There is no pre-established timetable. Many considerations influence the decision. "How soon?" remains an individual preference or choice, right, and prerogative to decide. Some are so shocked and distraught after the death of their spouse that the question of "How soon?" is moot.

Some say never. Others want to "start" their new lives as quickly as possible. They disdain being alone and admit needing someone in their lives to fill the void. They cannot fathom being without someone, citing the need for a level of intimacy, warmth, and close companionship, beyond the support provided by family and friends. These survivors claim to know their departed beloved would want them to move on, continue, and not be alone.

Some pause to assess the situation before deciding to do anything. They need to figure out where they are, where they want to go, what they want to do, and how they plan to get there. They collaborate and seek counsel and support of family and friends.

Some want a simple "time out" to pray, pause, and reflect, indicating there is no sense of urgency, citing the need to put their lives back together in a slower, logical, methodical manner – one step at a time.

Some will flex their newly found freedom to travel, undertake new projects, engage in new activities, or find new social groups. They move beyond the life style shared with their beloved. Their newly found freedom leads them on a quest for self-rediscovery. They may become preoccupied with their so called "bucket list".

"How soon" can be influenced by cultural custom, religious belief, family tradition, and individual mental and emotional status. Some statistics on the subject of re-marriage rates and speed differ between men and women.

Strategies for Developing New Relationships

Responding to the questions of "How do I develop new relationships?" and "What kind of relationship do I need or want?" can become a source of struggle for the widowed survivor. The dilemma encompasses how one readjusts from a precious, one person-centered relationship into an arena populated by many searchers, all on a similar journey with different motives, interests, and needs.

All potential relationships do not mean connecting with new people. In widowhood, as mentioned in Chapter 4.3: "Changes and Getting Overwhelmed", "we" became "I" and the related, social dynamics of relationships change. As mentioned earlier in this chapter, close friends and social acquaintances, with whom "we" previously associated, may be uncomfortable or ill-equipped to deal with "me". Their attitude and demeanor may change entirely. Survivors may soon and painfully learn there is no room for "me" in former social circles; thus they are ignored, avoided, and excluded without any prior warning or notice.

Some family dynamics may change. Family relationships may also differ for the widowed person with children and those who are childless (see Chapter 4.4: "Widowed with Children vs. without Children"). Some may be alone and without any family, or have family without ties or common connections. While the latter can be hurtful, the fact remains some people in today's society are unwilling to reach out and help. In today's society, family members may reside far away in different parts of the country. Distance impacts relationships. Some of the distance problems can be overcome by modern communications technologies, making it easier to keep in touch.

Varying circumstances and situations may spur some survivors to research resources in order to develop new relationships. Resources may be friends, support groups, church groups, travel clubs, volunteer opportunities, work, neighbors, relatives, and senior citizen centers; just to mention a few. Be careful, diligent, and open-minded when contemplating new relationships.

Internet Dating and Safety Tips

"Widowed Survivor Beware" of internet dating! Namely, become an informed consumer.

Internet dating has gained significant play, popularity, promotion, and acceptance. Internet dating is "big business". Commercials tout success stories with happy, fairytale endings.

Logically, there must be many success stories that have resulted from internet dating, because the concept is so well advertised, accepted, and received.

A few widowed survivors described internet dating as "risky", after reporting negative experiences with "predators", scam artists, and opportunists. This is not an indictment of internet dating, but reports of less than optimal experiences should be mentioned.

There is no intended or implied insinuation that internet dating is good or bad. I encourage potential internet daters to:

- Research the product and vendor.
- Ask questions and review the details of all contracts, agreements, and applications before signing them.
- Share only the personal information that you want to be known or made public. Be cautious.
- Safeguard private information – finances, income, phone numbers, and other sensitive personal data one would not routinely share.
- Initially, if you find someone you would like to meet, arrange to gather in an open, public place, with people around, during a busy time. First impressions are lasting impressions. Trust your initial instincts, impressions, and gut reactions.
- Correspond with a potential contact as long as possible before committing to a face-to-face meeting.
- Initially, be suspicious, skeptical, and untrusting. Get to know the other person as much as possible before sharing too much personal information. Ignorance is not bliss in internet dating situations; maintain a "caveat emptor" position.
- Be self-protective. Do not give your heart to the first smiling face or friendly voice you meet or hear. There are many fine, upstanding people who subscribe to, use, and claim positive experiences with internet dating sites.
- Approach each prospective contact with an open mind and judicious thinking. Do not presume that every contact or lead you may receive is someone who's in cahoots or out to get you. Similarly, every contact is also not the potential love of your new life.
- Exercise caution, not cynicism. But maintain the boundaries of familiarity and formality during the

"getting to know you stages". Namely, meet internet contacts with open eyes and open mindedness.

Stories abounding about internet dating reflect successes and horrors. Any assessment depends on the experience and perspective of the individual internet dater.

5.4 Where to Live

Kathy writes:

Deciding whether to stay in your current home or to move is a big decision for many widows and widowers. Should I stay here? Should I downsize to a smaller house and yard? Should I buy a condo? Should I rent an apartment? Should I move to another town to be near relatives? Should I move in with relatives? Should I move into a retirement community?

Because of the loss of the partner's income, for many widows there is a pressing financial need to move to a less expensive place as soon as possible. For others whose needs are not so pressing, it is a good idea to wait until the shock of the partner's death has subsided before making this major decision. Often advisors recommend waiting at least a year.

If you are considering moving for financial reasons, take into consideration the cost of preparing your house to sell it, realtor commissions, the amount to pay off your mortgage, and moving expenses. In a weak market, consider selling your first house before buying the next one, to avoid getting burdened with two house payments, even if you must move more than once. Consider downsizing your possessions ahead of time, to the amount that will fit into your new home. Otherwise, you must include in your calculations the cost of extra storage facilities needed after your move. If you are considering moving to a condo to reduce costs and simplify outdoor work responsibilities, consider the condo fees. Find out what it would cost for you to hire people to perform all the outdoor work for your current house, and compare the total to the condo fees.

For some people, moving will be emotionally painful. The home where you shared many memories with your partner, and your possessions in the home, may provide continuity and comfort. The location, your yard, your neighbors, your sense of safety, and the conveniences nearby might make it difficult to consider leaving.

Others might want to move in order to escape the memories of the loss. Your needs might have changed from those once provided by your current home. You might feel too isolated, or your house might be too large, too difficult to navigate, or too difficult to maintain. You might want to live near relatives, move in with children, or travel.

You might get useful information by talking to other widows and widowers about their decisions. You can compare notes about prices, amenities, and locations. Sometimes friends save expenses by moving into the same household. Get to know potential housemates well, before moving in with them. Agree upon household rules ahead of time, concur on a method for dealing with disagreements, and design a way for members to separate from the household if necessary.

Remember your pets when moving. Some condos and apartments have restrictions regarding pets. Make sure your pet will still get his or her needs met in a new place. Find out any legal restrictions regarding permits, health certificates, vaccinations, collars, and local ordinances. Ensure the safety of your pet during the move. Never leave a pet inside a vehicle on a hot day, because cars heat up to temperatures much higher than the surrounding air, which can be deadly to pets. Take your pet's familiar things and place them in the new home in positions similar to those in the old home. Play with your pet and reassure him or her, so that your pet will feel safe and remain calm. For many of us, our pets are our family.

John writes:

"Where am I going to live?" may seem rhetorical. Of course a logical answer is in my house! Where else would I go?

The question is not intended to be a joke or a pun, although at first it may seem so. For many, this question requires serious thought.

Truthfully, finances may strongly influence survivors' choices and alternatives. For some there is no question, "I'll stay where I live now. The place is paid off and I can afford to remain here. I like the neighborhood and I feel safe here." Others may relocate to a new place outside their current community, neighborhood, or abode; choosing to be closer to children, family, or friends. Some may seek a change of scenery or a move to somewhere they have always wanted to be. Alternatives available to the widowed survivor with children differ from the options available to the childless survivor.

Reasons for choosing to relocate or not depend on multiple and varied considerations, circumstances, and rationale. Some include:

"I really want to downsize. The place is too big and I don't want all of this responsibility and related expense."

"I cannot afford to stay here. Without my spouse's paycheck, my income is limited. I need to be in a place with more reasonable rent."

"This is not home anymore. This was our place. This is an empty place without my spouse. The next place has to be my place. I'm looking for a fresh start!"

"I need to move closer to family. I need to live with someone or in a place where I can be cared for. I don't want to be alone."

"I want to be closer to town, public conveyance, and other conveniences, since I am alone now."

"The weather here is too cold and I want to live in a warmer climate. I want to live near the shore (the woods, the mountains, etc.)."

"The kids are finishing up their last couple of years of school and all their friends are here. I don't want to uproot them."

Many factors will influence deciding on where to live.

5.5 Traveling Solo

Kathy writes:

My husband and I had planned to travel to many interesting places after we retired. He died before that could happen. Now if I travel, it must be without him.

So I travel much less now than I had planned. But I do take at least one trip a year. I go to a writer's conference in a beautiful part of the country, and then I travel a little while I am there. I choose a conference because there I can meet other people with whom I share a common interest, and I can attend workshops and talks on a topic that fascinates me. I have often thought about investigating the offerings of an organization called "Road Scholar", formerly "Elderhostel" (www.roadscholar.org). Road Scholar organizes classes and "learning adventures" for older adults in various locations. Participants include couples as well as single people, and working people as well as retired people.

So one option is to find interesting workshops or conferences and travel to them. Some conferences are designed specifically for widows. For example, Camp Widow holds a conference in different parts of the country three times a year. Refer to the "Resources" section of this book for more information. Another option is to find a trip or a cruise for single people. There are also Meetup groups whose purpose is to plan and take trips together. Sometimes I think about traveling to stay in spiritual retreat centers. There is a book called *Sanctuaries* (refer to the "Resources" section) that provides details about many retreat centers of various denominations, or without religious affiliation, where one might find refuge, peace, and perhaps even some spiritual direction.

One might even choose to travel alone, without the backdrop of a conference, workshop, retreat center, or group of other people. This can be difficult for some, and perhaps more difficult during early stages of grief. The absence of one's partner might be too much of a reminder of one's loss, and might be too emotionally difficult to bear. But there might be times when one wishes to make one's own retreat, and travel, and enjoy silence and contemplation.

You might find comfort by traveling with just a close friend or two, or close family member, to share the experiences. The companionship with someone you know well might help distract from the loss of intimate sharing with your partner.

Traveling solo is sort of a metaphor for what we must do in our lives now. Some of us plunge into the aloneness of it, seeking solitude and peace. Others seek companions for their journeys. Still others alternate times alone with social times. However we do it, traveling can be an opportunity for renewing ourselves.

John writes:

Death of a spouse challenges one to focus to reinventing themselves and determining how to survive. A common question is "How do I go about doing this transformation?" "The rules have changed since I was single." Earlier sections throughout this book discuss transitions, coping, moving ahead, changes, and initial adjustments. Every survivor has to adapt to an altered new reality. Some make the transition in an orderly fashion; others have to be convinced while they are being pulled and dragged; and, a few will choose to do nothing and want to be left alone.

Emotions, memories, questions, changes, and adjustments come into play immediately and simultaneously. The following lists are not an exhaustive litany, but rather a partial schema of "problems to be faced" when beginning the initial walk through the forest of widowhood.

Pains, Regrets and Memories:

Now I travel the road without the love of my life and face the challenges of moving on.

Regrets for things said or done cannot be retracted or undone.

Taking for granted our beloved would always be there upon return from an errand, a night out with the guys or gals, home after a hard day at work, an outing with the kids. Many expected their significant other would always be there; the new reality becomes crystal clear.

Memories of good times that will never be again.

Realization life has taken the terrible turn on the road to Neverland.

Picking up pieces of a shattered life in a world where two lived as "individuals" and as a "couple"; I and we, me and you, us and them.

Benefits:

I don't need permission to do whatever I want to do. I can make decisions without having to get a second opinion or consult with someone else; mine is the only one that counts.

I can come and go at my discretion. I can take off to whatever activity I want to pursue.

I can stay up as late as I'd like to and sleep as late as I want. My schedule is my own.

Changes:

I can do my chores when and if I want to do them.

I don't have to abide by old routines and things we had to do with our friends and family.

I'm my own person; I can choose to participate or just stay home.

Priorities may become reshuffled and schedules change.

I miss having someone nearby to talk over and discuss certain things.

Revisions and New Realities:

Things we did together, I now do alone.

Matters my mate used to handle are now things to be fitted into the new scheme of events. I have to pick up some new chores to keep myself, the place, and my life running smoothly. I have to pick up the slack; I don't have a backup.

I have to be open to re-educating myself to new duties and chores my mate just absorbed when we were a couple.

I write more things down, lest I forget. My built-in reminder service is gone.

5.6 Financial Survival

Kathy writes:

Earlier chapters of this book discuss pressing financial transactions that must take place immediately after the death of the loved one, and financial issues faced in the relative short term. This chapter discusses ensuring financial survival in the long term. Without my partner, what can I do to make sure that I will be taken care of in my old age? What if I need long-term care? What if I become incapacitated and decisions need to be made for me?

Go to the library, find some good financial books, and do some reading on financial concepts. The more that you understand about financial concepts, the better you can evaluate your financial advisor and the advice they are giving you. Choose a good, unbiased financial advisor, as described in the chapter "Urgent Transactions". Talk to the advisor regarding how to fund your old age. Here are some questions you might ask your financial advisor:

- Can you advise me on how to protect my assets against lawsuits?
- Can you advise me on how to minimize my taxes?
- What investments minimize my risk but still provide some income?
- What strategies can I use to protect against inflation?
- Should annuities be part of my strategy?
- What is my best strategy for social security choices?
- What is my best strategy for providing for potential long-term care needs?

Find a good attorney with expertise in elder law in your state. Consult with them to create the following documents, to be used in case you are incapacitated:

- Power of attorney for financial and legal matters
- Power of attorney for health care decisions
- Advance health care directive

For some widows and widowers, especially those with no children, the difficult part might be choosing the person(s) to serve in the two power of attorney roles. This might require discussions with brothers, sisters, nephews, or nieces. If there are no relatives, you might need to choose a very close friend, but someone you trust completely, who has only your interests at heart. Choosing now is better, rather than have a court make a choice later.

You should also discuss estate planning with an attorney. You might choose just to create a will, or you might need a trust, or you might need both. First decide what you want to do with your assets after your death, and then make sure that the documents created by the attorney fills your wishes.

Another task is to decide now on your funeral or memorial service and burial or cremation plans. There is some controversy about whether or not it is a good idea to prepay for these services. At least it would assist your survivors if you would document your wishes, including the source of money used to pay for them.

Planning now for financial survival in your old age is not always easy, and it is not inexpensive. But it makes matters much easier for those who survive you. And it provides peace of mind for you when you complete the plan.

John writes:

Finances rank among the greatest concerns the newly widowed survivor will tackle. (See Chapter 2.3: "Notifying People and Businesses", Chapter 2.4: "Urgent Transactions", and Chapter 3.2: "Living Within Your Means".) It's critical for one to grasp and become totally knowledgeable of their personal financial situation. Survival in today's world dictates the sooner the better because money still talks loudly.

Horror stories abound about surviving spouses whose financial picture was not as secure or as sound as they might have been led to believe. They were flabbergasted to find debt rather than savings and assets. In other cases, insurance policies thought to be in force had terminated or lapsed. Investments thought to be well managed and a foundation for financial security were liquidated or went bad. Sadly, a financial picture that was thought to be safe and secure was precisely the opposite of what the survivor believed or understood. It behooves the survivor to become aware and attuned to their financial situation with a sense of urgency and immediacy.

Newly widowed survivors are fiscally vulnerable. Crooks stand ready to exploit their vulnerability through scams, theft, deceit, larceny, fraud, or any dishonest and underhanded scheme they can devise. Some predators may include family, friends, and esteemed colleagues out to make a quick buck. Some of these bandits believe a widowed person may be a soft touch and exploit the situation, if they can, without hesitancy.

I have heard of some "victims" who were scammed by family members, especially by their children, who needed money to pay for substance or alcohol addiction, gambling debt, the results of bad investments, or in need of financial assistance. Requests for financial aid generally begin with a one-time plea and result in multi-year subsidies. The victim, wanting to be helpful, ends up draining and squandering their financial security on lost causes. The end result is financial ruin and disaster. What was intended as a one-time loan has become a perpetual bailout. In these situations "BEWARE".

If a survivor plans to provide any sort of financial assistance to anyone, consult an attorney. Have legally prepared contracts that specify length and terms of the loan agreement, interest rate, repayment period, performance expectations, collateral, and consequences in the event of default. Of course the simplest response is "NO."

1. Exercise discretion, due diligence, and take the time needed when rediscovering or coming to grips with your financial situation.

2. Gather all available pertinent information and documents, checking and savings accounts, insurance policies, income streams, recurring bills, debt, sources and uses of cash, assets and liabilities. All of this data becomes essential to developing a financial survival strategy. Do not rush the situation or the process.

3. Avoid shortcuts. They can present devastating consequences.

4. Secure advice, guidance, and assistance from trusted and well-known professional experts. The upfront costs are worth the expense in the long run to avoid becoming the victim of a scam or a bad deal. The widowed survivor needs to be in touch with and in control of their financial situation.

5. I believe, when asked to loan money to a friend or family, one becomes a banker or an ATM. Informal, casual relationships become very formal matters, unless you intend to give the money as a gift with no expectation of repayment.

As such, act like a banker, because there is no room for sentimentality. Many survivors have been robbed of their financial reserves by trying to be helpful. Protect yourself. Remember the monies you save may be your own.

5.7 Work and Life Purpose

Kathy writes:

Death brings us back to what is really important in our lives. Death is a reminder that our time here is limited. We need to accomplish what is most important, and we need to start now. All those things unrelated to life's most essential purpose suddenly appear trivial.

Death exposes what is trivial, but the death of a partner can also disrupt the sense of purpose. With a partner, there is a shared sense of purpose. When the partner dies, it's normal to feel lost. We can sense that we need purpose, but the hard part is finding out what that purpose is.

As I mentioned in previous chapters, when Dennis died I questioned whether I could go back to work. I questioned whether I could go on, for that matter. I soon decided that stopping work would increase my stress because it would be too big a change, on top of the huge change of the loss of my partner. I compromised by switching to part-time work. I decided to concentrate my effort on recovering, and healing myself. That became my purpose, for that time. That was all I could do, and it became my most important work. Our purpose can shift over time, and in the beginning of that time after the loss, our purpose is to grieve.

Sometimes it is possible to return to goals shared with a partner. Mary MacNeill, in her memoir *The Widow Down by the Brook,* describes her decision to return to building the house in the country that her late husband had started. I identified with MacNeill, because, after Dennis's death, I returned to the goal of building the house in the woods that he and I had talked about for twenty years. Working towards this goal has been difficult, but it has helped return me to some of the sense of purpose I felt with him.

Sometimes it is possible to return to one's own original purpose. From childhood, I felt that I was meant to write and to make music, and I am trying to return to that now. This book is one step in that direction.

Sometimes it is necessary to find new purpose. I know a woman whose new purpose became helping other widows and widowers to work their way through their losses. She reached out to many she didn't even know, and saved some people's lives. Many people find fulfillment in volunteer work. Focus on helping others can help distract from one's own difficulties. Others find new purpose in expressing themselves creatively, intellectual exploration, or adventure travel.

One's work might be part of one's life purpose, or it might be a means to support oneself, so that one must achieve purpose apart from work. Sometimes the death of a partner can shock the survivor into making a career change that shifts work closer to purpose.

Finding one's purpose is essential to healing for widows and widowers. Purpose is something larger than oneself that gives a sense of wholeness. That sense of wholeness is what we feel we have lost when our partners died. Finding purpose when one's partner has died can be a struggle, and it may take time, but it is the journey we must take.

John writes:

Widowhood enables the surviving spouse to define or redefine their work life and purpose. The tragedy of being widowed may lead one to question their purpose, especially in the wake of grief, bereavement, and mourning.

Survivors will question, "What is my life about now? My spouse and my family were the center of my existence, the core of my being. How can I put the pieces back together?" Concern arises when a survivor is unwilling, denying, or ignoring the relevance of their work and life purpose. Understandably, one may become dysfunctional upon the loss of their spouse. Such makes resiliency and getting feet back on the ground as quickly as possible critically urgent, especially when children are involved and require parental supervision.

Those experiencing difficulty getting back on track should actively pursue professional counseling, spiritual guidance, support group membership, or other professional remedies and interventions. Failure to reconnect with one's life purpose signals potentially severe problems such as chronic depression, emotional instability, physical ailments, or just plain "I give up".

The ability to delineate one's life purpose and work helps strengthen one's resolve to survive and continue. Facing reality clearly indicates that the survivor plans to continue and cope with life despite the loss of their spouse.

Remember not all widowed survivors are retirees. Many still have jobs, have become single parents, and remain the sole breadwinner in their families. For the working widowed survivors, loss of their spouse may mean a reduced income, unplanned expenses for illnesses and funerals, and the necessity to eke out a living in order to survive. Having enough money to live can be a challenge looming in the background. Assessment of work life and purpose can be useful in setting objectives and courses of action to survive after the death of a spouse. Survivors should seek needed assistance and guidance.

5.8 Are Goodbyes Really Goodbyes?

Kathy writes:

Before we experienced the loss of our partners, each of us probably had the idea that, after a period of mourning, widows and widowers "get over it" and "move on" with their lives, as before. I know I had that idea myself, before I actually experienced this loss. That idea is such a common myth in our society.

But the truth is that someone so much a part of us is never really gone. At least that was true for me. Seven months after Dennis's death, I wrote this message to a widowed friend:

> *He is such a part of me that I can never separate from, and I never want to. If I have a new relationship, it will never replace him. It seems as if everything I experience, everything in my house, every trail on my land in Indiana, every food I eat, every song I hear, reminds me of him. He is everywhere.*

That was a short time after his death, but I still feel the truth of that message even now. My emotions are calmer now, but he still permeates my life, and all I experience. This continuity is normal. It is not prolonged grief, not "complicated grief", as long as I am comfortable with it, and learning to cope. I cannot, and will not, pretend that someone I knew for forty years did not exist. He is part of my history, and always will be. All my experiences and sensations are colored by the time we had together. And it was a beautiful time.

Some who have lost a partner believe that they will meet again in an afterlife. Others experience dreams, visions, or signs of communication from their loved ones. For these people, death is not a final goodbye.

I feel that even without such beliefs or experiences, the history of closeness with a partner by itself can mean that he or she is always with us. Dennis is always in my heart. For me to say goodbye doesn't make sense. That doesn't mean that I can't have a new partner, or do new things without him.

Perhaps some widows and widowers need to say "Goodbye" to have a sense of closure, and to give themselves permission to accomplish new things without their partners. Some might not have experienced a good relationship, and so need a sense of closure even more. Other survivors might just have been very different from the one they lost, and might need to rediscover their own identity as part of their healing process, so part of this process requires saying goodbye. This is understandable. For these survivors, saying "Goodbye" helps them to let go.

Each of us is different. Some spent decades with our partners; others spent only a few years, or even months. Some shared many interests, tastes, skills, beliefs, attitudes, and experiences. Others were very different from their partners. Some had peaceful relationships; others were stormy. All these factors affect what works for each of us when we work through our grief processes. We share many experiences, but we each need to find our own way.

John writes:

Some argue that closure of the casket, an official death certificate, sprinkling cremains, sealing up the grave, and lack of a living spouse indicate death means a last goodbye.

But is death a final goodbye?

Why have I have chosen to discuss the matter? I believe goodbyes are not really goodbyes.

Widowed spouses continue to hold close the tangible and intangible relics of lives spent with their beloved. The deceased continue living on in survivors' hearts, minds, and memories. Remembrances and reminders of many possessions and items were previously discussed. The good times are headlined by stories, significant celebrations and observances, and family lore that evidence and document lives and times spent together.

There are tangible "things", accumulated as a result of sharing a life with another person. The "family" home, where the family grew and children were reared, landscaping, possessions, photographs, swing sets, additions and renovations to the original house are all reminders. These physically remain after the death of a spouse and do not represent "good-byes".

Children and grandchildren are reminders of "us". How many times have we heard grandparents reminisce and mention how much the "little one" looks like some particular member of the family? These are living testimonials, not goodbyes.

Many couples had special songs and they may have identified one as "our song". A life spent together is souvenired with special restaurants, movies, books, events, occasions, vacations, adventures, clothes, jewelry, furniture, trinkets, cards, pictures, and dates, just to mention a few. Such "things" consistently inundate and clutter the memory, making it hard for goodbyes to really be goodbyes.

Some have retained love letters, cards, and precious documents from the courtship days. These are part of a rich and precious past legacy. Are goodbyes really goodbyes?

Many religious traditions and cultures teach that life exists after death. Such beliefs emphasize reuniting with loved ones when life ends on this plane of existence. Many scientists, physicians, therapists, mental health providers, clairvoyants, psychics, clergy, mediums, and religious texts espouse the notion that life exists after death. Dr. Raymond Moody's book, <u>Life after Life,</u> was one of the first books written on the subject.

Some survivors report having had paranormal experiences that may have included physical contact, dreams, signs, and communications with their loved ones.

Again, this topic remains a matter of subjective, personal, and individual belief.

Others believe life ends at death. They affirm death is a final, conclusive goodbye, asserting there is no life beyond this earthly realm. They may be right, as the practical and forensic evidence proclaims, "Dead is dead."

I believe we do not say "goodbye", but rather say "so long, until we meet again."

5.9 Who Am I Now?

Kathy writes:

The first message I sent to anyone, only hours after Dennis died, stated, "I am now a widow." I remember how strange it felt to write those words. His death was such an unexpected shock that a great deal of time was required just to recognize that he had died. Time was required for me to realize that I was now a widow.

"Widow" has become part of who I am now. In the raw beginning, this meant that I became someone who belonged to no one, who had no family, no one to come home to, suspended in isolation. Eventually I reached out to find new family, by connecting more with my brothers, and with new and old friends.

Death pushed me to explore what I really want to be. Before Dennis died, I worked in the field of information technology, as an employee for someone else in an office. Now I am retired and self-employed, a writer, musician, gardener, and builder of a homestead in the woods. The work that I do now is closer to the work I have always wanted to do, for many decades. I worked on many fascinating projects in information technology, but now my work is more self-expressive. Now I spend more time outdoors, in the woods or in a garden, where I have always longed to be. There is still more I want to do to get closer to my dream, but I am moving in that direction.

I believe that death helps to strip away that which is not essential, because it makes apparent what is most important. At the same time, death is a deeply wrenching experience. When Dennis died, I kept saying that half of me had been ripped away, and that is exactly what I felt. I was just on the verge of retiring, and we had plans to build our dream house in our woods, travel, and have great adventures. We had planned our whole lives for this time. Now our plans were shattered. But I was shattered as well. Dennis was my soul mate. We shared the same dreams, the same interests, and sometimes it seemed that we shared the same experiences, that we could feel a piece of music together in the same way, or the experience of walking in a forest. The connection felt almost mystical sometimes. So when he died, the experience of aloneness was intense.

I had to find a way to live my dreams, but I had to do it without him. I found myself doing tasks I had never done before, or had done rarely, such as mowing the lawn, putting out the trash, repairing the cat's scratching post, dragging leaves back to the woods, and cooking. So perhaps I became more independent, of necessity.

In a similar way, I became more self-contained, from necessity. I feel more secure in myself. I feel grateful to Dennis for having shared his life with me, and I feel that somehow he has helped me find that sense of security, of inner peace.

Becoming a widow can result in identity crisis. You are no longer "wife" or "husband" or "partner". You are no longer half of a couple. Now there is no one there reflecting back who you are. You might have to try new things, a small step at a time, to find out what you can do, who you are, and what you want to be. Widowhood can be scary, but it can also be freeing. You might find out who you are all over again, and you might discover that you like that person.

You might connect with a new partner, or you might not. A new connection might not matter as much as it once did, if you feel peace within. If you do connect, your new relationship will not be the same as your old one. Each relationship is unique. You will still remember your lost partner, and you can still grieve and honor your late partner while building your relationship with a new partner. These two things are not contradictory. Love never dies.

John writes:

Is it delusional to believe, as widowed survivors, we have not changed since the death of our spouse? We know who we really are, don't we? Whether we recover from the death of our spouse remains another question.

Admittedly, since Nancy's death I am widowed, single, and quasi-surviving without the love of my life. I am alone. At times, my existence can be confusing, lonely, depressing, uncertain, and boring. At other times, I welcome getting out with friends, exploring new activities, not being bound by a schedule, sleeping in as late as I like, and being accountable to no one else but myself. However, I would forfeit my newfound freedoms to have my beloved Nancy back.

Challenges include standing on my own, doing the best I can, remembering the good old days, trying not to get submerged in the quagmire of the past, staying strong, keeping busy, occupied, and caring about what matters to me.

Many widowed survivors are battle-tested, sober realists who know things will never be the same again. We fully comprehend the notion that walking confidently into the future requires determination, resilience, stamina, and courage. Moving ahead is not a simple romp in the park. One may find it difficult to maintain the fine balance between independence, reaching out for support, and being an intrusive pest.

At times, I need and long for the company of others, even perhaps another one special person. I relish the prospect of companionship. I want to be happy and care free. But, at other times, I embrace solitude, being alone with my thoughts, and find comfort retreating to the safety of my sanctuary. When

I'm down, I migrate to a somber space within myself and have a pity party bemoaning the fact of "Why me? Why does God treat me so badly?" I ask, "Lord, where are you? Do you really care about me? I want to awaken from this terrible nightmare; but the nightmare is real."

At other times, I am happy, jolly, and pleased to be alive. I find myself doing things I never previously contemplated. The reinvented "me" has started reaching out, trying new adventures, and pursuing interests. I declined doing some of these activities before losing my beloved because I thought they were boring, foolish, or a waste of time.

Now I am a single widowed survivor. I have given some of the activities she suggested before her death a whirl – e.g., learning to play bridge, dancing, spending more time with friends. I have even tried some new things, which friends from my past life might consider uncharacteristic.

I enjoy helping others who may be experiencing difficulty. I find pleasure keeping up with friends. I like doing what I want to do when I want to do it. I have the options of undertaking or avoiding projects, accepting or declining invitations, or sitting out events in which I do not care to engage. I say "NO" without feeling guilty. "**No**" is a simple, clear, complete sentence without any need for explanation or justification.

I have become more of a curmudgeon, when I choose to be; an outgoing dynamo and social butterfly, when I choose to be; and a more tolerant person, when I choose to be.

I am stronger in my religious practice and spirituality – duly influenced by Nancy for over 34 years. I am cautiously optimistic about the future. I have not been alone in a long time. Being alone is scary and depressing as much as it is tolerable and embraceable. I'm no longer cock-fire sure or so dogmatic about many of the absolutes to which I vigorously clung, believed, and adhered to in my younger days. I am more prone to admit, "I don't know", or fess up to "maybe I was wrong", or "tell me more."

I am flexible about some things, willing to hear differing points of view, more tolerant of divergent beliefs, and more open to question, collaborate, or seek advice when and as needed. But there are still things about which I feel strongly and I will not compromise.

I do not feel the need to be in charge, to be in the lead, or to be the driver of the bus. I'm happy to be part of the group and help where I can. Actually, one is in a great position when they can opt to offer input, go with the flow, or walk away. I don't mind being a follower or just a member of the pack. If I don't like what's going on I can leave without any consequence.

There is grace in walking away from controversy, peace in avoiding confrontation, and courage to admit, "This is not my fight." Everything doesn't have to be an issue, much less my issue. Let others argue, debate, and jockey for power; I really don't need to do that anymore. I've been there, so what?

The haunting regrets of unfulfilled promises, things left undone, and alibis will last forever. But conversely, there is pride, joy, and consolation in the good, maybe even great things we jointly accomplished during our marriage. Happy memories are all I have left. We married for life, willingly stayed together for life with unwavering commitment, and deeply loved each other. Disastrous issues and tragedies we shared, and conquered, during marriage would have put many couples asunder. We survived the losses of children, financial setbacks, and illnesses. Conversely, we celebrated each other, children, grandchildren, promotions, and new adventures.

In widowhood we can sit and stagnate, live life voraciously to the point we burn ourselves out, or take each day one at a time and try to do the best we can. Remember yesterday is history, tomorrow is a mystery, and today is the present.

Who am I now? That's a good question. In some ways I'm still the same person; in other ways I've changed. In some cases I'm both richer and poorer. At times I feel stronger, at others weaker, and sometimes just numb, lethargic, and apathetic.

I'm independent because I have to be. Widowhood has been a difficult shift from being dependent on someone whom you loved, adored, and enjoyed sharing a lifetime, to being alone.

- I'm happy because I'm still walking on the green grass, but sad to be walking on the grass alone.
- I'm rich because I have some family and friends, but poor because my spouse and sons left me.
- I have mixed emotions about the uncertainty of the future. I am pessimistic because I face the future alone. I am optimistic because I have a few good old friends and a few new friends.

I've had to become many persons, face new situations, and perform tasks I never wanted. Roles I have played were unscripted; casted, but never on my radar screen. The unfathomed tasks needed to be done because they were inherent to my new role as a widower and were dictated by the demands of survival. Journeying alone, after spending many years with the love of your life, is devastatingly rough. You have to roll with the punches or the world will suck you in, chew you up, and spit you out in pieces. Trying to make sense out of the death of a spouse, while continuing to navigate the choppy waters, is much easier with the help and support of family and friends.

But the complex, unanswered question remains, who am I now?

Overall I'm still me. I've reinvented myself to become a traveler on my grief journey, play nicely with others, and live the rest of my life peacefully. Many survivors feel or experience similar pains, emotions, and shocks. But no one has walked along the path in my shoes, nor have I walked in their shoes. Many aspects of a grief journey are essentially similar and yet uniquely individual.

There was no dress rehearsal, casting call, or audition for widowhood. The script reflects a cold, brutal, final reality. As Sonny and Cher crooned, "The beat goes on."

May you experience healing, peace, and joy on your journey.

Resources

This section is a list of resources, including phone numbers, web resources, face-to-face resources, books, and films, to help the widow/widower, family, and friends, to survive and cope. These resources all existed at the writing of this book, but over time are subject to change, beyond our control.

Emergency
Of course, if your life is in danger, call 911. But sometimes you might just feel an intense need to talk to someone right now, although it is the middle of the night. There are hotlines that you can call anytime, 24 hours a day, just to talk, and there are chat rooms that you can join at any time of the day or night.

Hotlines
1-800-273-TALK (8255) is the phone number for the National Suicide Prevention Lifeline, but you do not have to be actually on the verge of suicide to call this number. Counselors are prepared to listen to any of a variety of issues, even just loneliness. They are available at any time, 24 hours, 7 days a week.

1-877-297-9436 is the phone number for the American Widow Project, 24 hours, 7 days a week, but it is for military widows only.

We searched for a general widows' hotline, but have been unable to find one.

Chat Rooms
A chat room can be a wonderful way to break through feelings
of isolation, even in the middle of the night. Chat rooms are
websites that allow you to communicate in real time with
others by typing text that is displayed to the others in the
"room", and reading what they type. It can be more satisfying
than forums because responses happen now, while you are in
the "room". One night I communicated at 2 AM with a few
widows from places as diverse and faraway as California and
Newfoundland.

At this writing, these are web addresses for some chat rooms:

http://widownet.org/chat02/

http://widowedvillage.org/ (click on the chat link)

AOL also has a widow/widowers' chat room, but it requires
that the participants subscribe to AOL.

Forums
A forum is a website that allows you to read others' messages
and post your own messages, but the "conversation" back and
forth is not in real time. You can post a message at any time,
day or night, for others to read and answer at a later time. So
it is not as immediately interactive as a chat room.

At this writing, these are web addresses for some forums:

http://www.dailystrength.org/c/Widows-Widowers/support-
group

http://www.griefhealingdiscussiongroups.com/

http://griefnet.org/

http://widowedvillage.org/forum

Support Groups

We have found grief support groups extremely helpful in overcoming the intense isolation we experienced after losing our spouses. A grief support group is a group of people who have all experienced the death of someone close, and who meet face-to-face regularly. Sometimes the group is moderated by a professional counselor, and other times it is moderated by someone from within the support group. Some grief support groups are designed to support those who have lost any friend or relative. You might find it more helpful to join a grief support group specifically for the loss of a spouse. Sometimes it is helpful to belong to more than one group, when more frequent support is needed.

To find a grief support group who meets near you, contact any of the following:

- A church
- A hospice organization
- A funeral home
- A web search for a list of support groups in your city
- A search of the Meetup website (see next section below)

Meetups

The "Meetup" website, at www.meetup.com, is a collection of clubs, or groups of people, focused on a particular interest, within a particular city. Anyone who pays an annual fee can host a Meetup. The host sets up a web page that describes the intention of the Meetup, and then the host posts meetings, along with the topic or activity, location, date, and time. Others can search for Meetup based on their city and their interests, and then sign up to receive notices and to attend face-to-face meetings. There are many topics of interest, and some Meetups are devoted to support for widows/widowers. It's another way to find a local grief support group, or to organize a new one. It's also a great way to meet new people interested in the same things you are interested in.

Conferences

Camp Widow is a weekend conference for widows and widowers, held three times a year in a hotel in a major city in the USA or Canada. The website is www.campwidow.org. The conference includes round table discussions, presentations, workshops, and a bookstore. Some financial aid is available. Everyone is very friendly, and it's easy to meet new people. It's an uplifting event.

Websites

The following is a list of websites and blogs dedicated to support for widows and widowers:

> http://abigailcarter.com/ -- blog created by author of the book *The Alchemy of Loss: A Young Widow's Transformation*.

> http://americanwidowproject.org/ -- organization for military widows.

> http://www.centerforloss.com/ -- resource for those who grief and for those who support them, authored by Alan Wolfelt, who developed the widely quoted Mourner's Bill of Rights (see http://www.centerforloss.com/2014/02/mourners-bill-rights/).

> https://www.foreverfamilyfoundation.org/ -- organization focused on research and education on the afterlife, as well as support for those who are grieving.

> http://hopeforwidows.org/ -- a blog and peer support group for widowed women, developed by widows.

> http://www.lostmypartnerblog.com/ -- blog written by two psychotherapists. Good resource, containing practical advice.

> http://www.opentohope.com/ -- website of the Open to Hope Foundation, dedicated to helping people find hope

after loss (not necessarily a spouse). Contains many articles and an area for posting and reading comments.

http://www.refugeingrief.com/ -- website and blog written by a grief counselor who lost her own partner, and whose approach acknowledges the raw intensity of grief, and the importance of validation from those who truly understand.

http://www.ripthelifeiknew.com/ -- blog written by Kelley Lynn, comedian, writer, actor, and performer, who describes her own loss in all its raw intensity, but sometimes uses very supportive and empathetic humor. Kelley gave an excellent presentation at Camp Widow at Tampa in 2014.

http://www.soaringspirits.org/ -- organization that sponsors Camp Widow, Widowed Pen Pal, Widowed Village Forum, and regional social events.

http://www.widownet.org/ -- an older website containing resources for widows/widowers.

The following websites are dedicated to those who have lost someone to suicide, not necessarily a spouse:

http://www.allianceofhope.org/alliance-of-hope-for-suic/welcome.html -- Includes a forum, and counseling resources.

http://heartbeatsurvivorsaftersuicide.org/index.shtml -- Heartbeat, a peer support group offering empathy and coping techniques to those who have experienced the suicide of a loved one.

http://www.oursideofsuicide.com/ -- Blog created by two young women who lost their fathers to suicide, but it also contains stories from those who lost a spouse to suicide.

https://www.soslsd.org/ -- Includes phone and email support, support groups in southern California, newsletter, and volunteer program.

http://www.speakingofsuicide.com/ -- Created by a therapist. Contains *A Handbook for Survivors of Suicide*.

http://www.survivorsofsuicide.com/index.html -- Includes a forum with a small annual subscription fee.

The following websites are dedicated to those who have lost a loved one to homicide, not necessarily a spouse:

http://www.novabucks.org/otherinformation/homicide -- NOVA (Network Of Victim Assistance), based in Pennsylvania. Contains an article in support of family members of victims of homicide.

https://rememberinghomicidevictims.wordpress.com/ -- provides emotional support and guidance to those who have lost a loved one to homicide.

http://www.vcvs.org/ -- violent crime victim services, based in Tacoma, Washington.

This website maintains a large directory of links to grief support websites, organized by the type of loss:

http://www.mygriefangels.org/Grief_Support_Directory.html

Websites for Friends of Widows

The following is a list of websites and blogs dedicated to those who are friends of widows and widowers:

http://friendsofwidows.blogspot.com/ -- blog focused on those who are friends of widows, and a community of those who wish to support widows, to connect and learn from each other.

http://www.huffingtonpost.com/megan-devine/death-and-dying_b_4329830.html --- an article entitled "How to Help a Grieving Friend: 11 Things to Do When You're Not Sure What to Do", written by a therapist who is herself a widow.

https://throughawidowseyes.wordpress.com/2011/02/08/to-the-friend-of-one-widowed/ -- an article within a blog, suggesting what to say and do, and what not to say or do, to help your widowed friend or family member.

Books

Aikman, B. (2013). *Saturday Night Widows*. New York: Broadway Books. The author, a young widow, tells the story of her experience in organizing her own grief support group. She tells the stories of five other widows, as well as her own, and their adventures together in remaking their lives.

Beischel, C., with Strom, K. (Eds.). (2002). *From Eulogy to Joy*. Herndon, Virginia: Capital Books. This is an anthology of essays, written both by those who grieve and by those with professional expertise on grief, over any loss, not only the loss of a spouse. It includes separate chapters on children's deaths, the death of parents, the death of spouses, mates, and ex's, and the loss of friends. It includes a chapter on children's perspectives on death. It discusses unusual topics such as the death of someone with whom you are angry, and unnatural deaths. It contains several chapters on resources for processing grief, such as spirituality, journaling, and support of others.

Deraniyagala, S. (2013). *Wave*. New York: Vintage Books. This memoir is the story of a woman who lost her parents, her husband, and her two young sons in the tsunami that hit the coast of Sri Lanka in 2004. The author spent years recovering, and she does not hold back her traumatic and negative experiences from the account. But by the end of the book, seven years later, it's evident that she is regaining her balance. The first part of the book might be difficult to read if your loss is recent, or if it resulted from a similar sort of event.

Dwoskin, H. (2007). *The Sedona Method: Your Key to Lasting Happiness, Success, Peace and Emotional Well-Being*. Sedona, Arizona: Sedona Press. This is not a book about grief, but a general book describing simple techniques for releasing emotions. It contains exercises that must be practiced to benefit from the book.

Ericsson, S. (1993). *Companion Through The Darkness: Inner Dialogues on Grief.* New York: HarperCollins. This is one of my favorite books. It's a set of essays written by a young widow, fresh in her grief. Each chapter is short and strikingly to-the-point. It is a very frank expression of her emotions and thoughts, including shock, disorientation, anger, rage, and humor.

St. Francis of Assisi. (1952). *Song of the Sun: From the Canticle of the Sun.* New York: MacMillan. Illustrated by Elizabeth Orton Jones. A beautiful picture book, written as a children's book, illustrating verses from St. Francis's Canticle of the Sun, celebrating the natural world and praising its divine creator.

Gilbert, S. (1997). *Wrongful Death: A Memoir.* New York: Norton & Company. This memoir tells the story of the unexpected death of the author's husband in the hospital, her grief and shock, the barriers she faced in trying to find answers to her questions, and her subsequent lawsuit for malpractice.

Gilbert, S. (2006). *Death's Door: Modern Dying and the Ways We Grieve.* New York: Norton & Company. This book draws on literature, memoir, history, and culture, to describe how we grieve. Gilbert is a professor of literature, so that informs her work, but she is also a widow, so this is not merely an academic treatise.

Guggenheim, B., & Guggenheim, J. (1995). *Hello From Heaven!* New York: Bantam Books. This is a collection of 353 accounts of after-death communication, not only with late spouses, but also with other relatives and friends who have died.

Jeffreys, J. Shep (2011). *Helping Grieving People – When Tears Are Not Enough: A Handbook for Care Providers* (2nd ed.). New York: Taylor & Francis Group. As the subtitle states, the target audience for this book is grief counselors. However, reviews suggest that it is easy for lay people to understand, and may be helpful both to those who are grieving and to friends and family members who wish to help those who are grieving. The book is the original reference for the often-cited Seven Principles of Human Grief.

Kelly, J., & Kelly, M. (2010). *Sanctuaries, The Complete United States: A Guide to Lodgings in Monasteries, Abbeys, and Retreats.* Bloomington, Indiana: iUniverse. This is not a book about grief, but is referenced in the chapter "Traveling Solo". Traveling to a retreat center might be a good way to find peace, and perhaps even spiritual guidance. This guidebook refers to retreat centers of different denominations, and some that have no religious affiliation.

Kennedy, A. (2001). *The Infinite Thread: Healing Relationships beyond Loss.* Hillsboro, Oregon: Beyond Words Publishing. This book is written by a psychotherapist who has taught courses and written on death, dying, and grieving. It is a practical book that contains chapters on communicating with one who is dying, connecting with the one who has died with dreams, letters, dialogs, and imagery, and reaching outward to friends and relatives. I found most helpful the chapter on setting up a sanctuary and opening to grief each day using that sanctuary.

Kübler-Ross. E. (1969). *On Death and Dying: What the Dying Have to Teach Doctors, Nurses, Clergy and Their Own Families.* New York: Macmillan. More recent editions are available. This is a classic, often-cited book by a psychiatrist who described stages of emotions experienced by terminally ill people, based on her work with dying patients.

MacNeill, M. (1999). *The Widow Down by the Brook*. New York: Scribner. This is a memoir written by a woman whose husband died while he was working to build their dream house in the countryside. She learned to become independent, and after his death, she finished the house and lived there for many years. This book was particularly inspirational to me, because my own husband and I had been planning to build our own dream house in the woods when he died.

Martin, J., & Romanowski, P. (1997). *Love Beyond Life*. New York: HarperCollins. This book includes many accounts of after-death communication, and documents the healing power of these experiences.

Moody, R. (1975). *Life After Life*. Covington, GA: Mockingbird Books. More recent editions are available. Classic book about the common elements of near-death experience, based on interviews with those who have experienced coming close to death, or being declared dead, and returning from the experience.

Moss, R. (1996). *Conscious Dreaming: A Spiritual Path for Everyday Life*. New York: Three Rivers Press. This is the best book on dream interpretation I have seen. It recognizes that the one who dreams is the best interpreter of those dreams, and provides techniques for drawing out the meaning from the dreamer. If you are interested in understanding dreams about your late partner, this is the place to start.

Oates, J. (2011). *A Widow's Story: A Memoir*. New York: HarperCollins. Joyce Carol Oates, acclaimed author of many novels, tells the story of her husband's unexpected death and her grief process. It is an excellent, well-written book, and I found it difficult to stop reading it.

Rehl, K. (2010). *Moving Forward on Your Own: A Financial Guidebook for Widows*. Land O'Lakes, Florida: Rehl Financial Advisors. This book was recommended to me by a financial advisor shortly after the death of my husband. It might be most useful to those who have little background in finance.

Rinpoche, Sogyal. (2002). *The Tibetan Book of Living and Dying*. New York: HarperCollins. This is a wonderful book that imparts wisdom about the nature of life and death, how to prepare for death, how to help those who are dying, how to help those who have already died, and how to help those who are grieving.

Rivers, J. (1997). *Bouncing Back*. New York: HarperCollins. Joan Rivers' husband committed suicide, so this author has an understanding of those special circumstances that add to the trauma. She makes many good practical suggestions for surviving and "bouncing back".

Roiphe, A. (2008). *Epilogue*. New York: HarperCollins. This memoir begins some time after the death of the author's husband. It includes flashbacks to her life with her husband, describes her coping now alone in her apartment in New York City, and tells the story of her adventures in dating new men.

Saltzman, N. (2012). *Radical Survivor*. Colorado Springs: WoWo Press. This book tells the story of a woman's loss of her husband and two sons in a plane crash, and the uplifting story of her strength and positive approach to survival.

Stang, H. (2014). *Mindfulness and Grief: With Guided Meditations to Calm Your Mind and Restore Your Spirit*.

New York: Cico Books. This book provides an eight-week program of exercises including meditation and other practices specifically designed for those who are grieving the loss of a loved one.

Staudacher, C. (1994). *A Time to Grieve: Meditations for Healing After the Death of a Loved One.* New York: HarperCollins. Written by a grief counselor, this book contains a set of short essays. Each essay starts with a description of a concern or worry of the grieving person, and then includes suggestions for dealing with the worry.

Vogel, G. (2007). *Choices in the Afterlife: What We Can Do and Where We Can Go after Death* (3rd ed.). Keene, New Hampshire: Choices Publishing. Gretchen Vogel is a psychic who describes what the afterlife is like, based on her own psychic intuition. The book is interesting, and much of it rings true, especially the idea that there are stages in the afterlife.

Articles

Carnelley, K., Wortman, C., Bolger, N., & Burke, C. (2006). The time course of grief reactions to spousal loss: Evidence from a national probability sample. *Journal of Personality and Social Psychology,* 91(3), 476-492.

Davidson, K. (2001). Late life widowhood, selfishness and new partnership choices: a gendered perspective. *Ageing & Society,* 21(3), 297-317.

Davidson, K. (2002). Gender differences in new partnership choices and constraints for older widows and widowers. *Ageing International,* 27(4), 43–60.

Elwert, F., & Christakis, N. (2008). The Effect of Widowhood on Mortality by the Causes of Death of Both Spouses. *American Journal of Public Health,* 98(11), 2092-2098.

Holmes, T., & Rahe, R. (1967). The Social Readjustment Rating Scale. *Journal of Psychosomatic Research*, 11(2), 213–218.

Koropeckyj-Cox, T. (1998). Loneliness and depression in middle and old age: Are the childless more vulnerable? *Journal of Gerontology: Social Sciences*, 53B, S302-S312.

Lynn, K. (2014). *An Invisible Hurt: Widowed and Childless.* http://www.ripthelifeiknew.com/2014/05/12/invisible-hurt-widowed-childless/ Last updated: May12, 2014. Accessed April27, 2016. Author's email: RIPTheLifeIKnew@gmail.com

Meekhof, K. *5 Things a Health Care Provider Should Not Say to a Widow.* http://www.huffingtonpost.com/kristin-meekhof/health-care-widow_b_7261612.html/ Last updated: May12, 2015. Accessed May 23, 2016. Author's contact: http://www.kristinmeekhof.com/contact-kristin-meekhof/

Redfoot, D., Feinberg, L., & Houser, A. (2013). *The Aging of the Baby Boom and the Growing Care Gap: A Look at Future Declines in the Availability of Family Caregivers.* Washington, D.C.: AARP Public Policy Institute.

Zhang, Z., & Hayward, M. (2001). Childlessness and the psychological well-being of older persons. *The Journals of Gerontology Series B: Psychological Sciences and Social Sciences*, 56(5), S311-S320.

Film

About Schmidt (2002), starring Jack Nicholson. The main character's wife dies suddenly just after he retires. The film shows him dealing with grief, surprising discoveries about his late wife, conflicts with his daughter, and feelings of his own uselessness. The film ends with some uplifting life lessons.

Inception (2010). A fascinating movie about a spy who enters other people's dreams to steal their secrets. The spy continues to meet his late wife in his own dreams. I really like the insights into this film expressed in this article: http://brilliantdisguises.blogspot.com/2011/01/inception-and-grief-documented.html.

The Descendants (2011), starring George Clooney and Shailene Woodley. This is a movie about a husband grieving the loss of his wife during her coma and death after an accident. It is a very emotionally moving film, with themes about the importance of family and natural heritage. When I first saw this movie, three years after the death of my husband, there was one scene that shook me to the core. This might be difficult to watch for early widows/widowers. It is an excellent film, and a couple of years later I did not find it disturbing.

Up (2009), animated film. This is a cartoon, but it is engrossing and epic, a serious and ultimately uplifting adventure story. Part of that story includes the death of the main character's wife, the love of his life, and his process of working through his grief.

Especially early in the grieving process, some of these movies can stir up emotions difficult to handle. Refer to http://widowsvoice-sslf.blogspot.com/2012/01/movie-ratings-for-widowers.html

Index

A

abuse, 119, 121, 171, 189
affair, 116, 117
American Widow Project, 118, 221

B

burial, 34, 38, 39, 62, 86, 124, 125, 204

C

Camp Widow, 199, 224, 225
celebration of life, 40
chat room, 222
complicated grief, 160, 162, 210
cremation, 34, 125, 204

E

Elderhostel. *See* Road Scholar
Ericsson, Stephanie, 128, 228
estate, 47, 48, 49, 50, 51, 62, 109, 139, 156, 204

F

forum, 123, 135, 222, 225, 226
Francis of Assisi, 90, 228
friends of widows, 3, 127, 149, 226
funeral, 2, 15, 21, 24, 34, 35, 38, 39, 40, 41, 42, 43, 45, 46, 47, 48, 53, 54, 55, 62, 65, 79, 86, 94, 118, 121, 123, 124, 125, 132, 135, 185, 204, 223

G

Golden, William, 83
grief journey, 4, 5, 22, 30, 76, 92, 97, 98, 134, 146, 147, 166, 167, 188, 219

H

health care provider, 149, 233
Holmes and Rahe Stress Scale, 103, 149
homicide, 118, 226

I

Internet dating, 176, 179, 181, 182, 192, 193, 194
introspection, 137, 138, 139, 140, 141, 144

J

Jeffreys, J., 74, 75, 229
Jones, Elizabeth Orton, 90, 228
Jung, Carl, 81

K

Kübler-Ross, Elizabeth, 75, 229

L

Lynn, Kelley, 109, 225

M

MacNeill, Mary, 13, 207, 230
meditation, 34, 68, 90, 91, 120, 137, 138, 139, 151, 232
memorial service, 2, 11, 34, 35, 36, 38, 41, 44, 55, 121, 173, 204
military, 38, 118, 121, 221, 224
Miller, Bonnie J., 163
Moody, Raymond, 213, 230
Mourner's Bill of Rights, 127, 224

Index

O

obituary, 2, 9, 34, 35, 38, 41, 42, 43, 64,
146

P

Posttraumatic Stress Disorder, 23,
30, 66, 67, 79
prayer, 6, 15, 29, 34, 36, 38, 90, 91, 92,
93, 138, 139, 140, 151
probate, 48, 50, 51
prolonged grief, 160, 161, 162, 163,
210

R

Rivers, Joan, 65, 231
Road Scholar, 199
Roiphe, Anne, 184, 231

S

Saltzman, Nancy, 164, 231

Sanctuaries, 199, 229
scams, 56, 57, 188, 192, 205, 206
Schumann, Robert, 84
Sedona Method, 100, 119, 120, 227
Shirley, Joan, 80, 175
Social security, 44, 45, 47, 51, 52, 59,
60, 103, 203
suicide, 78, 79, 80, 118, 120, 162, 221,
225, 226, 231

T

Tibetan Book of Living and Dying, 36,
231

V

veteran, 38
Veterans Administration, 44, 47
Vietnam, 16

W

war, 66, 118, 121

About the Authors

Dr. Kathleen J. Cahalan holds an undergraduate degree in psychology, master's degrees in education, psychology, and information systems, and a Ph.D. in information systems. She completed all work except the dissertation for a Ph.D. in psychology. She spent the last 35 years of her career in information technology, where she discovered ways to combine aspects of education, psychology, and systems in her work. Now she spends her time gardening, hiking in the woods, playing harp and ukulele, and writing.

Dr. John A. Cosco earned a Ph.D. in health services administration and management. He has master's degrees in education and management. He has held key leadership positions in hospitals and multi-corporate healthcare systems, consulted to healthcare and human service agencies, and taught at several colleges and universities. He is a Life Fellow of the American College of Healthcare Executives. He has written and lectured on leadership, organizations, patient-centric care, management and strategic planning. His recent work focuses on coping with mourning, grief and bereavement due to the deaths of spouses and children.

Made in the USA
Columbia, SC
25 September 2024